NOTHING BAD HAPPENS
TO GOOD GIRLS

Oregonian article
No More Prisons book
The Color Purple -pg 74
author Andrea Todd- pg 93
information for "Two Mothers"
        pgs 88
          76
          80-81
          84 - why this case was
                   publicized
          83

Michael Moore's commentary on case

88

NOTHING BAD HAPPENS TO GOOD GIRLS

Fear of Crime in Women's Lives

ESTHER MADRIZ

UNIVERSITY OF CALIFORNIA PRESS
BERKELEY   LOS ANGELES   LONDON

University of California Press
Berkeley and Los Angeles, California

University of California Press, Ltd.
London, England

©1997 by
The Regents of the University of California

Madriz, Esther,
    Nothing bad happens to good girls : fear of crime in women's
lives / Esther Madriz.
        p. cm.
    Includes bibliographical references and index.
    ISBN 0-520-20291-0 (cloth : alk. paper). —
    ISBN 0-520-20855-2 (pbk. : alk. paper)
    1. Women—Crimes against—United States. 2. Fear of
crime—United States. 3. Women—United States—
Psychology. 4. Women—United States—Attitudes. I. Title.
HV6250.4.W65M3625 1997
362.88'082—dc21   96-37659
                                                          CIP

Printed in the United States of America
9 8 7 6 5 4 3 2

To Steve,
compañero de luchas y aventuras

To my two children, Tuttie and Carlos,
for opening my eyes to the beauty of life
and to the power of unconditional love

To all the women and men who, every day, carry on their lives
resisting social injustices
and bringing hope to the world

To the memory of my parents, Esther and Luis Madriz,
who, although they never attended college,
instilled in me the love for education

Yo soy Dominicana, y vine a este país buscando estabilidad económica para mí, para mis hijos, porque mi país está en vías de desarrollo y éste es un país desarrollado. Pero, por qué es que para lograr un avance económico hay que enfrentar el peligro de asesinato, hasta de muerte? A pesar de mi miedo, yo tengo que trabajar de noche. Qué hago entonces? Me trago mi miedo.

I am Dominican, and I came to this country in search of economic stability for me and my children, because my country is on the road to development, and this is a developed country. However, why is it that to achieve economic advancement you have to face the danger of attack, or even death? In spite of my fear, I have to work during the evenings. So, what do I do? I swallow my fear.

Carmen, a twenty-four-year-old woman from the Dominican Republic who participated in a focus group in New York City.

Contents

Preface

According to the Bureau of Justice Statistics, U.S. Department of Justice, these are some of the highlights of crime in this country during the last decade of the twentieth century:

- In 1994, victims suffered 10.9 million violent crimes.
- These crimes included a half-million rapes and sexual assaults, 1.3 million robberies, over 2.5 million aggravated assaults, and 6.5 million simple assaults (1996, 2).
- The highest rate of violent crime victimization occurred among men, Blacks, Hispanics, the young, the poor, and inner city dwellers (1996, 4).
- The lowest rate of victimization occurred among white women (61.5 per 1,000) (1995a, 233).
- Black women had the highest rate of victimization among women (1995a, 233).
- Hispanics sustained a robbery rate about twice that of non-Hispanics (11 versus 6 per 1,000, respectively) (1995a, 233).
- Compared to those households with annual incomes of $15,000 or more, persons in households of less than $15,000 were three times more likely to be raped or sexually assaulted, two times more likely to be robbed, and one and one-half times more likely to be victims of an aggravated assault (1996, 1).

These statistics show that crime is, indeed, a serious problem in the United States. It affects everyone. But minorities and the poor are more likely to be the victims of violent crimes.

Our knowledge of crime, however, is not shaped by the official statistics. It is, rather, influenced by the personal experiences of ourselves and others and by cultural representations embodied in bedtime stories, fairy tales, media images, everyday conversations, code words, and polarized concepts of good/bad, black/white, men/women, rational/irrational, and victim/offender.

This book looks at the many ways fear of crime affects the lives of women in the United States. I do not mean to suggest, however, that women are the only ones affected. Most studies of fear of crime consider both men and women. I have also interviewed men. They have shared with me stories of how crime touches their lives as well, revealing their own terror of violent personal attacks, murder, and rape. This fear exists among all types of men, but particularly among African Americans, Latinos, and gays. Moreover, men's lives are affected—directly and indirectly—by the anxieties of the women who are their wives, mothers, girlfriends, daughters, partners, sisters, and friends. Although this is a book about women, it is intended for everyone with an interest in this subject. Some of the concepts and vocabulary may be new to readers, but I try to present them accessibly.

I have used focus groups and in-depth interviews to gain insight into women's everyday experiences and to uncover the ways they understand and deal with their daily fears and worries about themselves and their loved ones. Although I use official statistics to inform readers about the types, frequency, and likely victims of crime, I rely mainly on qualitative information to answer the question, Why? instead of, How many? In short, rather than report on the number of women said to be afraid of crime, I ask, Why is it that women are afraid of crime? What images are embedded in women's fears? How are these images constructed? Do these images reinforce existing structures of power? How?

The title of this work is inspired by a phrase my mother used to repeat to me: *Si eres una niña buena, nada malo te pasará* (If you are a good girl, nothing bad will happen to you). This saying illustrates the social and political control that fear of crime exerts over women's lives. I offer this book as a witness to such control, in the hope that it will help restore the reputations of some of the brave "bad girls" who refuse to let the fear of crime rule their lives.

Acknowledgments

My fundamental debt is to the many women who opened their lives to me, sharing their fears, anxieties, and worries as well as their hopes and dreams for a better world: one without fear. To them, thank you for your trust and confidence. I am especially grateful to Ruth Sidel, who, during one of our lively conversations at lunch in a cozy restaurant in New York City, encouraged me to write this book. Her unwavering intellectual and personal support have been and still are wonderful gifts to me. I also owe an intellectual debt to Lynn Chancer, who helped me to develop and clarify many of the ideas contained in this book. Her suggestions for improvement were always very much on target.

I am also indebted to many of my students at Hunter College, who challenged my ideas and shared with me the joys and sorrows of intellectual life. I want especially to mention Marcia Esparza, Carmen Rosario, Patricia Valadez, Raven Rowe, Rafael Hernandez, Yolanda Martins, Kristina Rodriguez, Ivelisse Rosario, Marie Chatergoon, Cassandra Ritas, Judy McGuire, Noema Ioffe, Lorraine Latchman, Katherine Ulanowsky, and many others who wrote magnificent papers on their experiences with fear of crime. Many of their ideas contributed extensively to the development of this book. At Hunter College, Pamela Stone, chair of the Department of Sociology, supported my research and granted me time to finish my dissertation and to write this book.

Rosa Del Olmo, Latin American criminologist, mentor, and friend, first inspired me to pursue my graduate studies in criminology. She introduced me to the critical approach in criminology twenty-one years ago, just when I was finishing my undergraduate education at the Catholic University Andres Bello in Caracas, Venezuela. As a woman and as an intellectual, she has been and continues to be a role model.

Walter Gove, the chair of my dissertation committee at Vanderbilt University, has also indirectly contributed to this book. He tutored and instructed me in academic rigor and excellence, encouraging me to give my best. During the difficult moments—finishing my dissertation while teaching a full load, attempting to publish articles in academic journals—he was always an inspiration and a reliable friend.

I have benefited from the work of many British, Canadian, and U.S. academic feminists who have conducted important research in the area of women, crime, and fear of crime: Elizabeth Stanko, Meda Chesney-Lind, Carol Brooks Gardner, Pat Carlen, Helen Benedict, Carol Smart, Jill Radford, Diana Russell, Lynn Chancer, Karlene Faith, Barbara Ehreinreich, Deidre English, Susan Brownmiller, Julia and Herman Schwendinger, and many others.

I am grateful to my family and friends, who always thought that I could write this book and with whom I obsessively shared many of my ideas. Their love, support, and tolerance made it possible for me to continue, in the face of many obstacles. To my husband, Steve Richardson, who read the manuscript and helped me clarify and develop some of the key concepts and arguments, I am also grateful. Thanks are also due my sister, Carmen Madriz, and my brother-in-law, Ken Barnes, who have always been there for me during the ups and downs of life; to my brother, Luis Enrique Madriz, for his courage in the face of many adversities; to my parents-in-law, Gene and John Richardson, for their steadfast support, care and love; and to my many wonderful friends, Otto Maduro and Nancy Noguera, Natasha Krinitzky, Gustavo Rojas and my *ahijado* Gaby, Beth Harding, Chris and Alejo Butters, my *compañera* Magaly Huggins, Patrice McSherry and Raul Molina, Anne Marie and Howard Harrod, Emma Matos and Tom Angotti, Joyce Hamlin, Ruth Prudente, Yaffa Schlesinger, and Pelaya Papazahari, for the countless ways in which they have enriched my life and supported me and my work. To all of you, my unconditional love and gratitude.

To Alison Turovitz, Danette Davis, Marilyn Schwartz, William Murphy, Jennifer Greiman, and Karen Branson, my gratitude for their meticulous attention to the manuscript, and to Naomi Schneider, my editor at UC Press, my appreciation for believing in my work and for her concern about women's lives.

Chapter One

Introduction

The Context of Fear of Crime

Here on 118th Street, not long ago, a lady, Miss Helen, was coming out of the grocery store with her seven-year-old grandchild, and the next thing you know is that she is laying on the sidewalk dead.

Yes, they shot her either from a window or . . . I don't know where.

It is not just being robbed that makes you afraid . . . It's just that people are . . . I don't know . . . they have some kind of sickness or something. . . . They seem to be mentally ill or something.

A lotta them are on dope. . . . It's a number of things.

I live in constant fear. I don't go out of my house unless I have to.

Especially during the night.

Participants in a focus group of six
African American senior women,
upper Manhattan, New York City

The past five years of my life have been filled with stories, conversations, and narratives of incidents such as the ones described by these African American senior women. I heard some of these testimonies while doing research for this book. But many came from informal conversations with thousands of women—students, friends, colleagues, family members. During long *sobremesas* (after-dinner chats), hiking trips, office hours, and class lectures, they have asked me, "What are you doing?" I reply, "I am writing a book on fear of crime and the way it affects women's lives." Regardless of the race, age, social class, or professional status of the interlocutor, my answer invariably strikes a common chord: "That is very interesting. I know what you mean. I can tell you the way it influences mine . . ." There follows a deluge of stories expressing the burdens, limitations, and feelings of powerlessness that fear of crime brings to women's lives. Some, like Marie, one of the participants in this study, add that despite their anxieties, "I have chosen to go on with my life, without letting the fear control me."

For women, the fear of crime has the unique ability to organize consent or unify views around "proper" gender roles: women cannot engage in certain activities because it is dangerous for them to do so, whereas men have no such limitations (Young 1996). Although people may claim to support equal opportunities for women in the workplace or in the use of public space, their real opinions are usually shocked out of them when they are confronted with the possibility of crime. The same person who emphatically states, "Women and men have the same right to walk the streets of America," may well say, in the next breath, "Well, doesn't she know better? She should not walk by herself at night. What does she expect?" Fear of crime touches deep-seated beliefs and evokes many assumptions not only about crime, criminals, and victims but also about "responsible" behavior for men and women. The major argument of this book is that fear of crime contributes to the social control of women by perpetuating the gender inequalities that maintain patriarchal relations and undermine women's power, rights, and achievements.

This book begins by discussing how fear of crime has become the number one problem for most people in the United States. It frames the study of women's fear in the context of past research, which has consistently found women to be more afraid of crime than men, and it explores some of the sources of this fear. It also deals with media depictions of crimes committed against women and their possible impact on women's fear of crime. The next chapter deals with two major questions: First, why are Americans more afraid today, even though official statistics indicate that crime is decreasing? Second, why are women more afraid of crime than men, even though their victimization rates are lower? This chapter also discusses the question of feminism in criminology. Chapter 3 shows how women express feelings of apprehension and fear when considering the possibilities of victimization, and it explores the content of those feelings. Chapters 4 and 5 discuss the opposing images of criminals and victims and show how their polarization contributes to women's fear of crime. The last chapter examines the various rituals women use to protect themselves against victimization and to lower their fear of crime.

This book relies on the experiences of Black, Latina, and white women. I present these women as they presented themselves to me—voicing complex, often conflicting views about a situation that deeply concerns and affects all of us. I show both the differences and the similarities in the way fear of crime affects and limits the lives and activities of women in different social positions. I have therefore conversed with senior, adult, and teenage women, as well as with women of various socioeconomic, racial, and ethnic backgrounds.

Using focus groups and in-depth interviews allowed me to reach a level of frankness which is seldom achieved by using survey questionnaires. Conducting groups in Spanish with both documented and undocumented women gave a voice to many who would not otherwise have expressed themselves. Holding sessions on the participants' own turf (an alternative school, an Upper West Side apartment, a suburban living room) made participants comfortable, yielding fascinating discussions. I invite the interested reader to see Appendix A: "How We Study Fear of Crime" for a more detailed description of the methodology.

Living with the Ghost of Fear

Fear of crime lurks in the American psyche. A 1994 *New York Times*/CBS poll shows that crime has replaced the economy as Americans' foremost concern. Many also worry that the country will be unable to effect a decline in violence over the next few years (Berke 1994a). Similarly, a study conducted by the Roper Organization in 1990 on a national sample of 1,984 individuals found crime to be the most serious problem facing their neighborhoods—above unemployment, child care, education, and other social issues (quoted in Bureau of Justice Statistics 1992).

Americans are altering their lives in an attempt to minimize their risk of victimization. A study of eight major U.S. cities indicates that 46 percent of people in the United States have changed their life-styles because of the fear of crime (Hindelang et al. 1978). Individuals try not to go out alone or at night; try not to frequent certain places, such as downtown areas of major cities and subways; and try to avoid contact with people who seem or look dangerous to them.

We all live under the spell of media representations of crime and violence. It is impossible to turn on our TV sets or browse through newspapers and magazines—and, more recently, the Internet—without coming upon a morbid story about the latest heinous crime, accompanied by a detailed report of the suspected criminal and the viciousness of the act. Like body counts during a war, New Yorkers get a nightly report of the number of murders that have occurred in the city during the day. The entire country's fascination with the double murder of Nicole Brown and Ronald Goldman vividly exemplifies media exploitation of crime, criminals, and victims. This fascination became an obsession during the trial of the person accused (and later acquitted) of those murders: the rich and famous football star O. J. Simpson, Nicole Brown's former husband. This media frenzy, feeding daily on our deepest fears in order to sell newspapers and TV advertising, is nothing new. But new technologies—satellite dishes, computers, and cable networks—enhance the media's power to exploit crime-related news by the almost immediate dissemination of such information to the most remote parts of the country and the globe.

According to official statistics, the crime rate in the United States is very high compared with the crime rates of other industrialized countries. A report from the Sentencing Project, a private, nonprofit research and advocacy organization dedicated to improving the justice system, shows that the U.S. murder rate is 11 times that of Japan, 9 times that of England, and 4 times that of Italy. The robbery rate is 150 times that of Japan, over 100 times that of Greece, and 47 times that of Ireland (Mauer 1991). The amount of violence directed against women in the United States is even more disturbing. The rape rate of the United States is 26 times that of Japan, 23 times that of Italy, 20 times that of Portugal, 15 times that of England, and 8 times that of France.

The two major official sources of information about crime in the United States are the FBI Uniform Crime Report (UCR) and the National Crime Victimization Survey (NCVS). The UCR compiles crime reports from police departments all over the country. The

NCVS asks a national sample of household members whether they have been victims of a crime during the six months prior to the survey. Since many victims fail to file a report with the police, the NCVS survey is considered a more accurate source of data than the UCR. In fact, it shows a far larger number of incidents than the UCR, which is usually the source quoted by the media and politicians. According to NCVS estimates, in 1994 only 36 percent of the crimes described by the victims were reported. Thus we know very little about crime; indeed most crimes go unnoticed by the police and the general public (Bureau of Justice Statistics 1996).

Both the UCR and the NCVS paint a gloomy picture of crime in the United States. In 1994, for example, the NCVS showed that for the roughly 100 million households in this country, 32 million property crimes were committed. Surprisingly, though, recent NCVS reports show that the crime rate (the number of crimes per 1,000 inhabitants), which had grown since 1973, peaked in 1981 and steadily declined until 1994! The rate of theft and household crime has continued a steady decline since the 1970s. The rate of violent crime increased between 1973 and 1981 and has remained stable since then. Between 1993 and 1994 the overall rate of violent crimes, as well as the rates of rape and simple and aggravated assault, slightly declined (Bureau of Justice Statistics 1996, 5, 6).

Contrary to the media image, most crime in the United States is property crime. According to the NCVS, in 1994 U.S. residents age twelve or older experienced a total of 43.6 million crimes. Of them, nearly 71 percent were property victimizations and 25 percent violent victimizations. Although murder is frequently reported by the press, giving us the impression that it is one of the most common crimes, it is statistically a rare event—according to FBI data 9 people were murdered per 100,000 in 1994, a slight decrease from the previous year (Bureau of Justice Statistics 1996). Moreover, although the majority of these murders are committed by acquaintances, the media focus on random homicides committed by strangers (Roth 1994). The probability of being murdered in the streets of America by a stranger is actually very low.

In spite of the decrease in crime, *National Law Journal's* second poll of public attitudes about crime found that between 1989 and 1994 the percentage of the respondents who said they were "truly desperate" about crime almost *doubled,* from 34 percent to 62 percent (Sherman 1995/96). This and other polls demonstrate that many people today live haunted by the ghost of crime, although the possibility of their being the victim of a robbery, an assault, or even a murder has slightly decreased in recent years.

The desperation leads many to seek a hardware solution. In a society in which the most serious human problem is used to sell goods, many people buy products to make them feel safer. Guns, mace, high-tech alarms, locks, "the Club," and self-defense classes are some of the enormous selection of marketable commodities we use to give ourselves the impression that we are protected against crime. Prominent among them are firearms. The Bureau of Alcohol, Tobacco, and Firearms estimates that "over 40 million handguns have been produced in the United States since 1973" (Bureau of Justice Statistics 1995b, 3). Not surprisingly, according to the Department of Health and Human Services, gunshot wounds are becoming a leading cause of death in the United States. For example, between 1985 and 1991 the number of motor vehicle–related deaths declined 10 percent, whereas the number of deaths by firearms increased 14 percent. If this trend continues, by 2003 more deaths across the nation will be caused by gunshot wounds than by automobile accidents ("Guns Gaining on Cars as a Leading U.S. Killer," *New York Times,* 26 January 1994, p. A-12).

People fortify their homes and persons in the hope that they can create a bubble of safety protecting themselves and their families against criminal victimization. In other words, public cynicism about the political system and its inability to control crime has driven many to privatize their protection (Berke 1994a). The use of private security has increased dramatically, from a $3.3 billion business in 1969 to $52 billion in 1991 (Cunningham et al. 1991).

Fear of crime and its impact on the general society have arguably become a problem as serious as crime itself (Clemente and Kleiman 1977). A criminal incident that has one or two victims can frighten scores of people and alter the way they live and the way they relate to other members of society. Fear of crime weakens the sense of community, decreasing social solidarity among its members and creating suspicion of strangers and erosion of mutual trust and cooperation (Liska and Warner 1991). Fear of crime paves the way for the emergence of more repressive attitudes toward criminals. Around the country politicians respond to the public's fury at criminals by making time behind bars harder than ever. Recent legislation has curtailed basic amenities. The 1996 federal appropriations act, for example, cut access to weightlifting, selected videos, and coffee pots. Recent California legislation eliminated prisoners' visitation rights. The prison expert Mike Quinlan, director of the Federal Bureau of Prisons, warns, however, that "if inmates aren't kept busy when you take away all those activities, they will find something to do with their time, and it probably will not be in the best interest of staff trying to monitor their activities" (Nossiter 1994).

Politicians capitalize on people's fears. Distancing themselves from "liberal politics" under the flag of "law and order," they blast each other for being too soft on crime. During the 1996 presidential campaign Bob Dole and Bill Clinton fought hard to co-opt the crime issue. Dole carried the law-and-order theme to a tent serving as a jail in the Arizona desert, where he was hosted by Maricopa County Sheriff Joseph M. Arpaio. Arpaio has won his reputation for being hard on crime by promoting chain gangs (Nagourney 1996, A13). President Bill Clinton did something unusual for a Democratic presidential candidate: he talked about crime more than his Republican opponent. His tough stand on crime even won him the support of the largest police organization in the country (Purdum 1996, A14). In 1994, women politicians generally lost voter support because they were not seen as being tough on crime ("In 1994, Vote for Woman Does Not Play So Well," *New York Times,* 3 October 1994, pp. A-1, B-10). Building on this view to foster his political advantage, California governor Pete Wilson publicly accused his female opponent, Kathleen Brown, of "lacking the courage" to be tough on crime and illegal immigration (Toner 1994).

Fear of crime has resulted in public demand for tougher and more repressive criminal justice policies in the belief that they will make us safer at home and enable us to walk the streets of our cities without worrying about being mugged, raped, or killed. Expenses associated with crime and criminal justice agencies have increased substantially during recent years even though crime rates have declined. In 1992 the U.S criminal justice system cost taxpayers over $93 billion, with about $41 billion directed to police and $31 billion to jails and prisons

(Bureau of Justice Statistics 1995a). Even in the midst of economic austerity, cuts in social programs, and budget balancing, the U.S. Congress responded to public fears by passing, in 1994, an anti-crime bill allocating an *additional* $30.2 billion. This measure will put 100,000 more police officers on the nation's streets over six years, it provided $8.8 billion for construction and operation of prisons, it expanded federal death penalties to cover about sixty offenses, and it requires a mandatory life sentence for a person convicted of a federal crime who has been convicted of two previous felonies—the famous "three strikes and you're out." This means we are cutting our social programs to expand police departments and to build more prisons. The politics of law and order has eroded the more liberal agenda on crime—prevention, rehabilitation, alternatives to incarceration, abolition of the death penalty. Moreover, the return to retributive justice masks the reality of crime control: public safety is unrelated to the severity of punishment or to the number of police officers on the streets (Platt 1994a). Studies clearly indicate that neither enacting harsher penalties nor increasing the number of police officers on the streets has any significant effect on crime (Currie 1985; Reiman 1995).

The Social Construction of Crime

The study of crime can be approached from different perspectives—specifically, the *objectivist* perspective and the *social constructivist* perspective. The objectivist approach takes as a given the existence of crime as a social problem. Objectivists maintain that by using official statistics, sociologists and criminologists must study the extent of the problem, its causes, and its possible solutions. For example, Jerome Manis (1974), one of the representatives of the objectivistic school, defines social problems as those conditions identified as harmful to society, but does not discuss how these conditions are defined or who has the authority to identify them. Functionalists, such as Robert K. Merton and Robert Nisbet (1976), also follow the objectivist approach by defining social problems as violations of norms, dysfunctions, value and norm conflicts, and social disorganization. According to Merton, crime is a consequence of the lack of opportunities to attain the social goal of economic success. The solution to crime is to remove institutional barriers preventing equal access to societal goals. The traditional Marxist perspective is likewise consistent with objectivism in that it defines as a social problem any condition that harms large segments of the population, such as racism, sexism, exploitation, and oppression (Liazos 1982).

The objectivist approach to crime is the traditional, or most conventional, view. It assumes that everyone agrees that crime is evil and people know right from wrong. Crime is considered objectively wrong because it is a violation of the law, the ultimate reflection of society's moral values (Goode and Ben-Yehuda 1994, 66). The problem with the objectivist view is that it disregards the fact that what some people consider to be criminal or wrong may not be deemed criminal by others. According to some individuals, for example, homosexual relationships should always be considered wrong, because they violate God's principles, according to which heterosexual relationships are the only moral sexual relationships (some representatives of major faiths support this argument). To others, however, homosexual relationships are as legitimate as other relationships. Similar observations can be made with regard to abortion. The Christian right, for example, sees abortion as a sin and a form of murder. Other groups, such as the National Organization for Women, deem it a matter of women's right to choose and to control their bodies.

From a social constructionist viewpoint, however, crime is considered a much more complex phenomenon. When studying crime as a social problem, constructionists take into account how, why, and by whom the "crime problem" is defined; why certain behaviors are criminalized and not others; why some acts committed by groups of people are defined as more harmful to society than others; why certain categories of persons are more likely to be seen as victims. Constructionists attempt to understand the symbolic value of crime in general and of specific crimes in particular for various socioeconomic, ethnic, and gender groups. The "problem of crime" is examined in the context of the needs of the groups who use it to foster their political and moral agendas (Jenkins 1992). Social constructionism takes into account the economic, social, and political characteristics of the groups who have the power to define certain behaviors as social problems. They also examine the relationship between the likelihood of being considered deviant or criminal and the relative powerlessness of people such as women, members of minority groups, and the economically disadvantaged (Ben-Yehuda 1986; Currie 1968; Erickson 1966).

Although social constructionists consider statistics important to the study of crime, they also see statistics as socially constructed because many crimes are excluded from the official records and because the numbers are influenced by political agendas and, particularly, by law enforcement activity. For example, if the government decides to launch a war against drugs, the result may be an increase in drug arrests among certain groups of people. Rather than reflecting an actual increase in drug consumption, sales, or trafficking among these groups, however, the increase in arrests reflects a political decision and its consequent implementation.

Social constructionism does not deny the reality of crime. Women, the poor, and members of minority groups are especially affected by the prevalence of crime in their homes, workplaces, and communities and by the possibility of becoming the next victim. Nevertheless, crime must be understood as socially constructed.

This book follows a social constructionist approach. In spite of the news media portrayals, the incidence of violence in the United States today is not unprecedented. In fact, our current levels are no higher than they were during the early 1930s and the early 1980s. Why is it, then, that fear of crime has reached unparalleled levels? Why is it that survey after survey shows crime as the number one concern among U.S. residents? What is the symbolic value of crime and fear of it in the United States? In a society in which multiple hierarchies based on class, gender, and race prevail, could it be that crime and fear of crime mirror these social hierarchies, reproducing the dominance of certain groups and the subordination of others—such as women and members of minority groups—and helping to set limits and impose controls upon their lives? Is fear of crime, at least in part, a *displacement* of other deep-seated fears, such as the economic anxieties that many Americans face during a time in which job stability is rare and wages are stagnant?

Fear of Crime among Women: The Paradox of Fear

Since the late 1970s fear of crime has been of paramount concern in criminology and victimology. Articles dealing with the issue abound in academic journals and books. Their findings consistently show that women and the elderly are more afraid of crime than men and the young (Clemente and Kleiman 1977; LaGrange and Ferraro 1989; Ortega and Myles 1987; Skogan 1987; Stafford and Galle 1984; Warr 1984). Even when the objective level of exposure to crime is low (for example, in lower-crime neighborhoods), women and older individuals are substantially more fearful of crime than men and younger persons (Baumer 1985). Furthermore, women are more likely to alter their behavior because they fear being victims of a crime (Stanko 1990, 15). A survey of selected cities shows that while 52 percent of women reported that they have changed their behavior for fear of crime, only 27 percent of men expressed similar changes (Garofalo 1977).

Victimization rates are lower among women and the elderly than among men and the young (Bureau of Justice Statistics 1995a). These two groups, however, express more fear of being victims of crime (Stafford and Galle 1984). The contradiction between the victimization rates and the levels of fear among women and the elderly is one of the most perplexing issues in criminology. It has come to be known as the "paradox of fear" (Warr 1984, 682). It is explained, in part, by saying that fear of crime is *irrational:* it is out of proportion to the objective probability of being victimized. This idea is reinforced by findings showing that the crimes the general public fears the most— crimes against persons or violent crimes—are in fact less likely to occur than property crimes.

Different factors are used in attempts to explain this apparent contradiction between victimization rates and fear of crime among women. According to some, gender differences in fear of crime reflect differences in strength and body size: women are seen as physically more vulnerable than men because, on the average, they are smaller and less able to defend themselves against physical aggression (Hindelang et al. 1978). Others argue that fear of crime among women may be related to the fear of rape, which for many women is the most terrifying criminal offense. In the United States, as well as in other cultures such as those of Latin America, warnings about sexual molestation are an important part of the socialization of girls. Girls are told "Sit like a lady," "Keep your legs together," "Keep your skirt down," and "Avoid talking to strange men" because if you do not, "Something bad could happen to you." Warnings vary from vague insinuations to open comments on the dangers of rape and sexual molestation (Riger et al. 1978). Thus women's socialization may increase the perceived seriousness of this crime, leading to a heightened sense of weakness and vulnerability and provoking considerable fear of rape even at lower levels of objective risk. Some suggest that the fear of rape may build up and "contaminate" many areas of women's lives, making women afraid in many social situations. As Margaret T. Gordon and Stephanie Riger state, "Most women experience fear of rape as a nagging, gnawing sense that something awful could happen, an angst that keeps them from doing things they want or need to do" (1991, 2).

None of these explanations reach the core of the problem. In spite of the vast amount of literature on fear of crime, we have just begun to grasp the full dimensions of the issue, especially in regard to women's fear. Criticisms have been raised in relation to past studies. Many of them use survey research methodologies, some employing national samples and some employing samples of one or several cities. Although surveys can give us a broad description of some social phenomena, including fear, they are problematic. Some of them underrepresent population groups, such as Black and Latina women, for whom the issue of fear of crime might be especially important, given their lack of social and economic power in U.S. society. My own experience with surveys leads me to conclude that minority women are indeed underrepresented (Madriz 1992). Such underrepresentation makes it difficult to know whether there are differences between white and minority women—Black and Latina, among others—in their level of fear or in the factors associated with it.

Many of these surveys attempt to measure a complex phenomenon, such as fear of crime, by means of a single question (Ferraro and LaGrange 1987). Some surveys use vague or simplistic types of questions to measure fear of crime. For example, one of the most common questions asks people how safe they feel walking alone in their neighborhoods at night. This question does not mention crime. Some older people may be afraid of walking in the dark for fear of falling or because of poor eyesight. In addition, this question refers only to the neighborhood, ignoring other social domains where crime may occur, such as the workplace or the home, where most of us spend more time. Studies of fear of crime in those places, however, are uncommon.

Another criticism of past studies is that the great majority of articles written in academic journals on fear of crime and women ignore domestic violence. The fears of many women and the policies aimed at reducing those fears—such as safety tips given by police departments and security telephones on university campuses—assume that most crimes against women are committed by strangers in public spaces. However, most crimes against women are committed by someone inside their social networks or in the "sanctity" of their own homes by men acquainted with the victim (Stanko 1993, 1991, 1990). Curiously, the relation between domestic violence and fear of crime has been neglected. We do not know, for example, whether a woman who is the victim of intimate violence or violence committed by her mate is also more fearful on the streets.

With very few exceptions, research on fear of crime has been carried out by middle-class male criminologists of European-American descent. This research has two important limitations. First, as previously stated, it fails to address differences between different categories of women. Second, it is often framed within the predominant positivist tradition in criminology, which focuses on individual attributes, such as the age, gender, or socioeconomic status of individuals, and the association of these variables with fear of crime. Most studies ignore wider social structures in which criminal incidents or fear of them takes place. Consequently, very few studies show an understanding of how race, class, and gender *relations* influence fear of crime or how such fear affects the lives of women of different racial/ethnic and socioeconomic backgrounds. In brief, the sociostructural context in which this fear occurs has been systematically ignored, with the exception of the work of a handful of U.S. and British feminist criminologists who have looked at the fear of crime and the way it limits women's lives (Gardner 1995; Green et al. 1991; Hanmer and Saunders 1984; Riger et al. 1978; Stanko 1990).

The everyday reality of many women is that we live under a self-imposed curfew, feeling that it is dangerous to walk the streets of our cities—or even of our suburbs and rural areas—after dark or to exercise our right to use public space (Gardner 1995; Walklate 1990). Without a doubt most would feel safer with a security guard protecting the entrance to their building (so they did not have to enter through a dark, unprotected hallway) or with a car to drive to and from work (so they did not have to take public transportation) and an electric garage door that could be opened from within the car by means of a remote control (so they did not have to walk five flights of poorly illuminated stairs, leading into their apartment). Lacking these amenities, poor women limit their activities. For example, Rosa, a sixty-five-year-old, lower-class Latina woman who lives in the area of Washington Heights, New York City, talked to me about her curfew:

I do not go out after dark. If I have to buy milk or I have to go to the grocery store, I wait until the next day. I rather do not drink milk than risk my life. I do not take any chances. I am old and don't have insurance. If I get hurt, who is going to take care of me? No way.

Thus poor and minority women seem to be more afraid of crime than middle- and upper-class white women (Gordon and Riger 1991). Class and racial differences play a role in women's fear of crime, and these differences have been consistently overlooked. Most research on fear of crime has approached the issue as if it existed in a political, economic, and social vacuum, neglecting to relate it to the social disadvantages that most women, especially women of color, occupy in a predominantly white and male-centered society such as the United States.

The possibility of violence and the fear it produces are fundamental elements in the control of women's lives. Thus, differences between men and women in the level of fear of crime can be, at least in part, explained by dominant images that reflect structural gender divisions and present women as comparatively vulnerable, weak, powerless, and passive and men as forceful, strong, powerful, and active. Those differences between men and women are presented as "natural," having their origin in biological differences—the implication being that they are based on unquestionable or "scientific" truths. Nevertheless, recent studies show that even factors presumed to be strictly biological, such as body size and physical strength, are strongly influenced by diet and physical activity (Andersen 1993).

From birth, social practices differentiate boys and girls. The names that we are given are marked by unmistakable gender expectations: girls' names are supposed to be representative of such virtues as passivity, sweetness, beauty, and goodness: Glory, Joy, Iris, Belle, Candy. Boys' names symbolize intellectual skills, determination, and courage: David, Arthur, William, James, Peter (Slater and Feinman 1985). Women are encouraged to be "lady-like," and ladies do not perform tasks that are physically strenuous. Boys are encouraged to be strong and to engage in sports and other activities that develop their physical strength and involve physical contact with other individuals. Women are frequently portrayed as physically and socially vulnerable and therefore as easy targets of crime and male violence.

In Susan Brownmiller's words, "Even before we learn to read we have become indoctrinated into a victim mentality" (1975). The stories and fairy tales that are read to us, usually by our mothers in the safety of our bedrooms, are filled with images and symbols of women or girls as victims of crimes committed by male figures. For Brownmiller, the story of Little Red Riding Hood is typical. A "good girl" is sent into the woods to take food to her sick old grandmother (a typically female nurturing activity). After lurking in the shadows, the "bad wolf," a strong, dark male figure, attacks the two women, who are swallowed by the beast without any resistance on their part. Another male figure, the courageous, strong, white huntsman, cuts open the stomach of the beast, rescuing the two frightened women.

Women's fears are shaped by images suggesting that the "woods"— a metaphor for unfamiliar places—are dangerous for girls and that women are vulnerable to violent male attacks and at the same time subordinated to men and in need of their protection. Many fairy tales teach us that men are our ultimate saviors. They rescue women who have fallen under a spell, such as Sleeping Beauty—who is awakened from a long dream by the sweet kiss of the handsome Prince—or have been abused by malevolent stepsisters and stepmother, like Cinderella, whose suffering ends thanks to the love of Prince Charming. The Cinderella story is particularly interesting, given the symbolism of the Prince desperately looking throughout the kingdom for the perfect woman, the one with the smallest foot—symbol of fragility, delicacy, weakness, femininity—to fit the crystal slipper.

The fear of crime, and specifically the fear of male violence, not only perpetuates the image that women are powerless, weak, and more vulnerable than men but also feeds into the notion that women and men are not entitled to the same rights: women should not and cannot go places where men can go; women cannot engage in activities which are open to men; women should wear "proper" attire so that they are not molested by men; and since women must protect themselves and their children from criminal victimization, they had better stay home and be "good girls." Further, the fear of crime reinforces the subordinate role of women: if a woman wants to be safe and protected, she had better be accompanied by a man.

The Media Depiction of Crimes against Women

Crimes against women are often misrepresented by the media. The frequency and the type of crime against women reported by the press usually distort the reality of where, when, and by whom women are more likely to be victims of crimes. Consider the criminal cases in the United States receiving the most media attention in recent years: the pool-table gang rape of a woman in New Bedford, Massachusetts, the rape case against William Kennedy Smith, the "preppie" killing of Jennifer Levin by Robert Chambers, the gang rape of the Central Park jogger, the killing of Carol Stewart by her husband Charles Stewart, the kidnapping of twelve-year-old Polly Klaas in California, and the murder case against O. J. Simpson. One gets the impression that most of the victims of crime are women, especially white women. Certainly, crimes in which the victim was not a woman have received attention, such as the killing of an African American youth, Yusuf Hawkins, in Bensonhurst, New York City; or the Howard Beach incident, in which a teenager was killed by a car while trying to evade an angry mob—in both of which cases race played a major role—or the bizarre serial killings committed by Jeffrey Dahmer. Nevertheless, violent crimes committed against women receive disproportionate emphasis in media representations about crime, criminals, and victims.

In spite of the fearsome images presented to us by the media, the overall victimization rate for women in the United States, as presented by the NCVS, is lower than for men: in 1994 the rate of victimization per 1,000 persons twelve years of age and older was 61.7

[handwritten marginalia: But what is reported? What is defined as crime?]

for males and 45.1 for females (Bureau of Justice Statistics 1996). A woman is one-third as likely to be murdered as a man. Furthermore, in spite of all the messages suggesting that women are safer at home, women murder victims are more than ten times as likely as men to have been victims of intimate violence. In 1992 about 75 percent of violent crimes committed by lone offenders and 45 percent of those committed by multiple offenders were perpetrated by someone known to the victim (Bureau of Justice Statistics 1995c). While media images present women as likely victims of strangers, the reality is that women are more likely to be victims of crimes committed by someone they know. Women are asked to stay home to protect themselves against crime, and yet a woman is much more likely to be assaulted at home than in the streets. In fact, about 86 percent of the victims who were killed by spouses were killed at home (Bureau of Justice Statistics 1994a).

Media images of women as victims vary along a continuum. At one end of the continuum we have the "good but stupid woman" (because of the she-should-know-better mentality), such as the Central Park jogger, a white middle-class woman in her late twenties, raped by a "wolfpack" of Black and Hispanic teenagers in Central Park, New York City. One of the first questions raised in the aftermath of the rape was, "How did she dare to be in the park at night?" (Benedict 1992). The twenty-eight-year-old investment banker was raped, according to many, for being in a place where women should not be—a public park—especially after dark (the rape occurred between 10:00 and 10:55 P.M.). After the rape and murder of a Brazilian woman, Maria Isabel Pinto Monteiro Alves, also in Central Park, the Guardian Angels handed women joggers a leaflet: "Female joggers beware. If you choose to enter the park without a partner, you will be like Bambi in hunting season, ENDANGERED. If you insist on defying the odds, then train to become a Rambolina and be ready to defend yourself. After dark! Be smart! Stay out of the park!" (McLean 1995). The imagery is indisputable. Women are compared to Bambi, a sweet and vulnerable fawn, terrified of the shadows of the woods and threatened by the male hunters. Since the implication is that women, like Bambi, cannot defend themselves, the recommendation is to retreat, forgoing another activity, and to "be smart" and stay out of the park.

In other words, if you do not stay out of the park, you are stupid and it is your fault if you are raped or killed.

At the other end of the continuum of media images of female crime victims is the "bad woman," such as Carol Ann Artutis, whose decomposed body was found on September 20, 1994, in a long-haul trailer alongside the Hudson River in the West Village in New York City. According to the press, Artutis was a runaway girl, always in trouble, hanging out with the wrong crowd, a victim of her passions and sins.

A friend of Carol Ann Artutis reported to the *New York Times* that "she was so haunted by fears of sexual assault that she regularly wore triple layers of underclothes" (Treaster 1994). This quote characterizes another feature of the media representation of women's victimization, what Dianne Russell has called "making violence sexy" (1993). In many instances the news media present violent crimes committed against women as entertainment, trivializing the impact that this violence has on the victim, her family, and the rest of society.

In the case of rape, according to Helen Benedict (1992), the media tend to eroticize the crime by following many of the popular myths in their reporting. Among those common myths are "rape is motivated by lust," "rape is sex" or "women provoke rape," "women deserve to be raped," and "women like to be raped." Even the words used to describe the crime reveal the inability of the press to understand the crime of rape and its implications. For example, in the case of the Central Park jogger, news accounts used terms such as *fondling* and *exploring*, rather than *grabbing* or *seizing* or other words that better express the ferocity of a sexual assault (Barak 1994a).

Entertainment is also filled with images of violent crimes. "If it bleeds, it leads" seems to be the motto of the entertainment industry. Hollywood films as well as TV dramas, soap operas, and miniseries bring murder, robbery, rape, and assault into our homes. According to estimates, 25 percent of prime-time television is devoted to crime-related themes (Surette 1992). In 1991, of all movies made for television in this country, 50 percent presented women as victims of one type or another (Elshtain 1995, 52)—in many cases as helpless victims of crimes committed by men.

Catalina, a twenty-year-old woman from Puerto Rico, shared with me the following narrative:

I came from Puerto Rico to go to college in this country. The first night I spent in the U.S., I watched a movie of a fairly young man getting acquainted with women from college campuses. After getting to know them and having conversations with them, he just raped them. I watched this movie with my mother. She probably thought that I was not fearful enough with the movie, because she went along to tell me how difficult it is to live in New York. According to her, women were very easy targets of crime—young women, especially, because of their physical attractiveness and careless ways in the streets. To her, young women are more in danger because they do not realize how men could take you and rape you, even kill you. Well, it was then when I opened my eyes and experience to the development of another sense—fear.

Catalina's words reflect how the entertainment media influenced her own and her mother's fears. Women, "especially young women," are "easy targets of crimes" committed by men who have complete power over them: they can "take you," "rape you," "even kill you." The absence of any possibility of response and the passivity when confronted with male violence expressed in this narrative suggest that women lack control over their lives and face many disadvantages in their everyday exchanges with men.

The idea of women as victims advanced by the media and supported by a masculinized ideology that identifies men as permanently strong and women as permanently weak nourishes women's fears and, paradoxically, contributes to their disempowerment. As Jean Elshtain suggests, the image of woman = victim embedded in the fear of crime limits women's ability "to see themselves as citizens with rights and responsibilities" (1995, 51). Fear of crime teaches women that some rights are reserved for men, such as the right to use public places, to take a walk at night, or, as one of the participants of this study said, "even [to go] alone to a restaurant or to a movie." Although such places are supposed to be open to all, women's access to them is often hampered by the fear of criminal victimization and by the possibility of sexual harassment (Gardner Brooks 1995). Many women do not even consider going alone to these places a viable option.

Chapter Two

The Manufacture of a
Good Girl

What I do to feel safe is try to "chameleonize." You know, I
do like the chameleon does. I try to be like everybody else,
act like everybody else, dress like everybody else. I mean, I
follow the rules and blend with everybody around me. I
use sneakers, try sometimes to appear more masculine
wearing baseball caps and baggy clothes. I try not to call attention. I feel that the more feminine you look, the more
likely you are of becoming a victim.

> Rosemary, a twenty-one-year-old
> African American woman who lives
> in a town in upstate New York

Why are Americans so afraid of crime? Why has their fear increased
in recent years even while crime rates have decreased? Why are
women more afraid than men? Why do some women, such as Rose-
mary, try to "chameleonize," to "blend," to look more masculine? Are
there some social gains derived from the panic produced by crime? Is
it, perhaps, that the current gender, class, and racial structures of
power are reinforced by such panic?

In the book *Policing the Crisis* Stuart Hall and his colleagues provide a theoretical framework for answering the first two questions
(1978, 135–6). They argue that the public discourse surrounding
crime and criminals serves as an "ideological conductor," deflecting
criticism away from the state agencies that have failed to deal with
such pressing social issues as unemployment, poverty, and inequalities of class, race, and gender. Instead people blame those they per-
ceive to be socially "dangerous" or "threatening" for the failure of the
state to solve these problems. It also justifies repressive polices aimed
at controlling these categories of people by defining them as "out-

laws" (Young 1996). There is nothing new about this argument. Major studies in sociology and criminology show how crime and its control provide a rationale for regulating and disciplining the behavior of various sectors of the population, especially minorities, the unemployed, and the poor (Greenberg 1977; Jankovic 1977; Quinney 1974; Rusche and Kirchheimer 1968; Spitzer 1975).

Americans do indeed have reasons to be afraid. Poverty is on the increase in the United States. During the last decades profound changes have occurred in the economy. Deregulation of corporate activity, "trickle-down economics," wage stagnation, and massive layoffs combined with cuts in social programs have resulted in a widening of the gap between the rich and the poor. For example, between 1977 and 1992, Jeffersonian ideals of America as the land of equality and opportunity have been challenged as the poorest tenth of the U.S. population saw its after-tax income reduced by 20.3 percent, while the richest tenth gained 40.9 percent, the upper fifth percentile gained 59.7 percent, and the single richest percentile gained 135.7 percent (Piven and Cloward 1993). A recent *New York Times* article reports that from 1968 to 1994, the last year for which complete data are available, income inequality has accelerated. Today, the gap between the rich and the poor is wider than it has been since the end of World War II (Holmes 1996, A-1). Cuts in social programs have further increased the levels of poverty, eroding some of the protections previously afforded to the poor. The U.S. Census Bureau estimated that 36.9 million persons—or 14.5 percent of the U.S. population— were living in poverty in 1993. The government, however, sets the poverty line at $14,335 a year for a family of four (U.S. Department of Commerce 1994). If we set the poverty line at a more realistic level, the number of those defined as poor would increase. The government has also managed to present unemployment numbers that are deceptively low because they exclude many who are working part time, are underemployed, or have to work two or three jobs to make ends meet. Furthermore, the threat of layoffs haunts those who had once believed themselves protected against unemployment because of their education and relatively privileged status.

Additionally, the United States has seen its position in the world market eroded by the competition of other economic superpowers such as the nascent European Community and Japan. Predictions indicate that the next generation's way of life will probably be worse than our generation's. Many American communities are plagued by a multitude of problems, from poverty to crime and from racism to drugs.

Powerful conservative politicians and groups—such as the Heritage Foundation, the Urban Institute, the Center for National Policy and others—have been successful in presenting welfare programs—and of course the poor, minorities, and immigrants—as a major drain on social resources and as a major contributor to a variety of social maladies, from spiraling poverty to moral deterioration and from teenage pregnancy to crime and delinquency. The inability of American institutions to deal with these problems has provoked widespread cynicism in the population. During these times of crisis, crime—and fear of crime—channel the expression of public anxieties away from the government's inability to deal with pressing social problems. Some groups serve as "scapegoats," displacing popular anxieties toward those who become convenient targets of society's fears (Hall et al. 1978).

American politics has frequently made such use of "enemies." Among some of the most recent were communists: millions of children in this country grew up learning to fear invasion from the Soviet Union. Since the demise of the Soviet Union, however, communists are no longer considered much of a menace. The impulse to look for enemies is nevertheless still very much alive. The current enemies, or scapegoats, however, are no longer international but domestic: immigrant groups, welfare recipients, teenage mothers, minorities. "They" are the most current source of America's fears.

Episodes of flagrant racism reflect the current mood in some of America's most important institutions, in an increasing number of U.S. political leaders, and in large sectors of this country's population. We have witnessed the videotaped assault on Rodney King by a group of police officers in Los Angeles; the audiotaped interviews of former Los Angeles police detective Mark Fuhrman during the trial of O.J. Simpson, in which he openly used injurious and derogatory words against African Americans, Jews, and women; the anti-immigration laws in California sponsored by Governor and ex-presidential candidate Pete Wilson; and, more recently, the burning of Black churches in the South. These episodes mirror prevailing attitudes toward those considered "outlaws" or just beneficiaries of scarce resources perceived by many to be the exclusive patrimony of "real Americans"—whatever that means in a country of immigrants.

Scapegoats Wanted

Two of the preferred scapegoats for politicians and sectors of the American public are immigrants and teenage mothers. Our interviews revealed images of immigrants as responsible for Americans' problems, especially crime. This notion was mentioned in particular by some of the participants in one of the focus groups with white elderly women, whom I interviewed at a senior center on the Lower East Side of Manhattan, in New York City. Gene shared the following views:

The whole problem is the kind of people that you have in this country today. When my parents came . . . that type of person was different. Now, we have people that do not have respect for themselves and that is the whole problem. They are the criminals.

Although Gene did not mention it openly, her suggestion is that "new immigrants," perhaps a code word for dark-skinned immigrants—Latinos, people from the West Indies—are the "whole problem." They are seen as responsible for most of the crime. Moreover, although she shared with the rest of the group that she is on welfare, Gene was very emphatic when she said:

They just want to come to our country and live on welfare. They do not want to work. All they want is to live off of us. That is why they commit crimes. They are too lazy to work.

Pam and Pat, two elderly, working-class white women who participated in the same group discussion, raised their voices and moved their hands in a very passionate way as they concluded:

You had different kind of people 20, 30, 40 years ago. Today you have garbage and that is the difference. They are not taught right from wrong. They have no respect for anybody. And as long as they have no respect for anybody, that's it.

Extending our arms to everybody. Come here and we'll feed you! [lifting her arms toward the ceiling]. That's why we have so much crime. Golden shrine. . . . Do you know? Wrong! That is the whole problem.

This emotional depiction of criminals presents in an ideological "package" several intertwined images: criminals are new, dark-skinned immigrants; lazy, poor, dirty; wanting to live off of "us"; garbage; on welfare; and disrespectful of others. Although prison statistics are not the best source of information on the characteristics of criminals—since some studies show that minorities are more likely to be arrested and sentenced than whites who commit similar offenses—they are one of the few ways we can begin to know about immigrants and crime. According to a survey of state prison inmates conducted in 1991, about 4 percent, or 1 in 23 inmates, were not U.S. citizens. Of those, 45 percent were in prison not for violent offenses but for drug-related crimes (Bureau of Justice Statistics 1992, 3). As these numbers show, 96 percent of the persons incarcerated in state prisons are actually U.S. citizens. Therefore, the belief that most criminals are immigrants is unsupported by available data.

Paradoxically, a recent Gallup Organization poll shows that in New York City immigrants are more afraid of crime than native New Yorkers. They are also more likely to have been victims of crimes (Friedman 1993, 4, 99). Anti-immigrant sentiments, however, are common-place today. In some cases, these sentiments are expressed in criminal actions against foreigners. Bergen County, New Jersey's local newspaper, *The Record,* recently reported several criminal incidents against undocumented Hispanic immigrants. In Fairview and Cliffside Park, two quiet suburban towns in northern New Jersey, teenagers have been attacking illegal immigrants, who report that they are living under siege. The attackers "count on the immigrant fear that reporting the crime to the police would result in deportation." An unidentified immigrant from El Salvador told *The Record* reporter: "I do not go out at night. . . . My black hair, my dark eyes, my skin—they'd go after me." One of the attackers, a nineteen-year-old, reported: "They haven't learned that when they get asked for money, they can't get stuck up about it. You have to turn it over, man." The attacker, who travels from the Bronx to the Fairview–Cliffside Park area every day to visit his girlfriend, continues: "Hey, this is no big deal in the Bronx. Mexicans get cleaned out every day over there. It's just tough luck" (Llorente 1995, A-1, A-12). Fairview and Cliffside Park police acknowledge that the crimes are not isolated incidents. They are rather part of a pattern of attacks against Latinos who do not speak English, because they are believed to be illegal. The attitudes of the two police departments toward the attacks differ sharply. The Cliffside Park police are conducting a campaign to spread the word that illegal immigrants who report crimes will not be turned in to the Immigration and Naturalization Services (INS). On the other hand, Fairview's police director said that although he wants illegal immigrants to report the crimes, he feels he must turn them in to the INS (Perez 1995, C-1).

Interviewees also considered teenage mothers responsible for many of today's maladies. Rose, an elderly woman who lives in the suburbs of northern New Jersey, commented to the group:

Children having children. That is the problem today. These young women do not understand that many of their children are going to be the criminals of tomorrow. They haven't even finished high school when they get pregnant. And, of course, they have to drop out, get on welfare and . . . of course, they cannot raise a child alone. And the fathers are out of the picture. And who pays for all of this? Us! [pointing to all the members of the focus group with both hands].

Rose's views are not unique. The image of pregnant teenage women on welfare as the cause of many of society's problems, including crime and drug addiction, has become a dominant theme in everyday conversations and in the political arena. Not surprisingly, the Clinton administration has launched a campaign against teenage pregnancy. This effort, however, ignores many of the realities in the lives of these women who are the target of so much fear and rage. The majority of them have been victims of childhood sexual abuse, usually inflicted by adults. In addition, a 1991 national study of 300,000 teenage mothers conducted by the National Center for Health Statistics showed that 67 percent had been impregnated by men older than twenty and that men over twenty-five are responsible for the pregnancies of more than four hundred teenagers daily! This is an indication that the demonized teenage mothers are actually the wrong target of American fears (Males 1994, A-15).

Perspectives on Crime and Women

Criminology has been a masculinized discipline (Smart 1995; Young 1996). Since its inception, the focus of study has centered on crimes committed by males. As MacKinnon (1987) points out, even studies dealing with equality and inequality place men at the center. Women enter into the criminological discourse only to be compared to men, as the "negation of masculinity" or as "Other" (Young 1996). Klein (1995) quotes a variety of sources throughout the history of criminology which have evaluated and characterized deviant women as masculinized monsters (Lombroso 1920), insensitive and lacking moral values (Thomas 1907), envious of men due to lack of a penis (Freud 1933), promiscuous (Davis 1961), and manipulative (Pollack 1950). These images have hardly changed, in spite of more than a century of development in the discipline.

Popular images of women as criminals are not far from those depicted at the outset of criminology. Flora, a teenage Latina student, told me during one of the interviews in a neighborhood school in Brooklyn, New York:

I rather deal with a man. Girls today are worse than men. They do not care about nothing. If they want your gold, they can kill you . . . for nothing. It is like if they do not believe in nobody. They do not have feelings. All they care is about themselves. I am scared of them.

Gloria, a participant in the same group, added:

All you have to do is read the newspapers or watch the news on TV and see how women have become worse than men. Remember that woman? What is her name? . . . The mother who killed her two babies. [Susan Smith?] Yes . . . I believe that's her name. She is a monster. . . . The worst. . . . A man won't do something like that. I wish they would do the same thing to her that she did to her kids. Lock her in the car and let her drown in the lake.

When women commit crimes, they are seen as monsters, much worse than male criminals because they go against strong, stereotypical images of how a woman "should be." Susan Smith, for instance, violated the image of the mythical mother, the ultimate representation of genuine, unconditional love and care. When the reality of a crime shatters such stereotypical images, the public reacts with outrage and vindictiveness.

In contrast to these popular preconceptions, most recent developments in criminology have focused not on an abstract concept of morality but on social realities. The work of conflict criminologists such as Chambliss and Seidman (1971), George Vold (1958), Richard Quinney (1974), and Steven Spitzer (1975), among others, deals with the economics of power, showing how wealthy and politically well-connected groups influence legislation and the implementation of justice in their favor. Rather than reflecting moral values, the legal system is shown to reflect the values and beliefs of those with the power to have their views embedded in the law. The control of the legal apparatus by middle-class white interests explains, for example, why today the law establishes harsher penalties for the possession of crack—a cheaper form of cocaine—than for the possession of powder cocaine—a more expensive form of the same drug. The typical image of a crack dealer is a lower-class, African American male standing in front of a housing project in an inner-city neighborhood. The typical image of a cocaine dealer is that of a white male who sells his drugs in front of a bar in a suburb. Crack is the drug of choice for the poor and minorities and cocaine of the white, middle-class professional. Possession of five grams or more of crack requires a mandatory minimum sentence of five years in prison. For cocaine, however, the five-year mandatory minimum applies to possession of 500 grams or more. The same drug, different penalties according to socioeconomic class and race (Clymer 1995, A-18; Dwyer 1994, A-2).

During the 1970s conflict theory evolved in the work of socialist feminists dissatisfied with the lack of attention to gender hierarchies in earlier work (Firestone 1971; Mitchell 1971). They claimed that Marx and Engels, as well as conflict and Marxist thinkers, did not consider the sexual division of labor. The laws, they argued, not only reflect the interests of the economic and political elites, but they also mirror gender divisions. Consequently, a pure economic analysis does not fully address the dynamics of gender differentials. In the field of criminology, therefore, gender differences are evidenced both in the superior economic and political power of men and in the perspective that predominates in the legal system.

Take, for example, the masculine bias at evidence in regard to rape victims and women who kill their abusive husbands. Rape is the only crime in which the victim's actions have to be judged to demonstrate lack of consent (Carlen 1994; MacKinnon 1993, 1987). Just picture a person who is the victim of another crime, such as burglary or automobile theft, having to justify why she had her TV set sitting in the middle of the living room or her computer in the office on top of the desk, or her car parked on the "wrong" street! In the case of women who kill their abusive husbands, only recently and in a handful of cases have a few judges begun to take into consideration the psychological trauma and the terror suffered by an abused woman when dictating their sentences. Still, many get sentences of fifteen years or more (Lewin 1994).

The recent case of a Maryland man, Kenneth Peacock, illustrates the influence of men's values and views on judicial decisions. Mr. Peacock, a thirty-six-year-old truck driver, was caught in a storm in February, 1994, while traveling from Pennsylvania to Florida. He called home to inform his wife Sandra that he would be arriving late, but got no answer. When he came home around midnight, he found his wife in bed with another man. After drinking and arguing, the truck driver shot his wife in the head with a hunting rifle. He pleaded guilty to voluntary manslaughter, but Baltimore County Circuit Court judge Robert E. Cahill—who asserted that he did not want to send Peacock to prison at all—sentenced the murderer to a mere eighteen months incarceration. "I seriously wonder how many men married five, four years would have the strength to walk away without inflicting some corporal punishment," the judge said. Judge Cahill's words reflect the common belief that if a man walks away from a situation like this, he is not a real man (Lewin 1994).

Crime, Unruly Women, and Social Control

Most work done in the area of crime and social control equates the so-called threatening populations with poor, unemployed, and minority men. Only since the 1970s have some studies attempted to include women among the groups that society would wish to restrain. Some studies of "witchcraft," for example, deal with the social control and stigmatization of "deviant" women and are indeed relevant to the topic (Szasz 1970). From the late Middle Ages through the Counter-Reformation in western Europe, uncounted numbers of people were tortured and killed as witches. Conservative estimates range from 200,000 to 500,000 witches sentenced to death from the early decades of the fifteenth century until 1650. Although men, children, and even entire families were also burnt, 85 percent of those executed were women (Goode and Ben-Yehuda 1994). Research shows that torturing and burning "witches" was a way of repressing and controlling women who were different, who challenged the traditions that placed men and their institutions in ultimate authority. In 1484 the Catholic church issued the *Malleus Maleficarum,* which stated the church's position on witchcraft, establishing that it stemmed from women's carnal lust, which was "insatiable" (Dworkin 1974). The charges leveled against witches included copulation with the devil, removing men's penises to be used in sacred rituals, stealing sperm from sleeping men, and devouring newborn babies (Ehrenreich and English 1978).

Witch hunts, as many authors explain, were a way to establish the patriarchal authority of the church and the medical profession over sacred and secular matters. They were directed toward women who "infiltrated" areas of knowledge or wisdom that were supposed to be the patrimony of men, such as healing, providing birth control, administering medicines to ease pain, and aiding women during delivery. To the physicians and religious authorities, these healers or wise women were usurpers attempting to erode their monopoly of knowledge. Consequently, they needed to be controlled (Ehrenreich and English 1978).

In the United States, toward the end of the seventeenth century, around twenty persons, including some men, were also tried as witches. Tituba, the kitchen slave from Barbados; Sara Good, the village hag; and Sara Osburne, a high-status woman of dubious reputation, so magnificently brought to us by Kai Erikson's *Wayward Puritans* (1966), are only predecessors of today's "witches." Witches scare but fascinate us. They are different, they are daring, they shatter our images of normality, they test society's limits and boundaries. American audiences filled movie theaters to see Meryl Streep's representation of Clara—the clairvoyant in the movie version of the magic realist novel *The House of the Spirits*—a Latin American witch in traditional Chilean society, who is afraid of nothing, immunized "forever against terror and surprise" (Allende 1993, 74). Is it only a coincidence that Clara was afraid of nothing, as writer Isabel

Allende reports? Are witches afraid of nothing? Is this why they are so frightening? Is this why they need to be controlled, limited, restricted, ostracized, terrorized? Are such women included among the threatening groups because they break established norms and social boundaries?

During one of the focus groups with African American homeless teenagers, ages sixteen to nineteen, whom I contacted through a community organization in New York City, three of these young women observed, "I don't worry about nothing," or "nothing scares me," or a similar phrase. Following are the comments of Ivette, Clara, and Mary, three of the participants in the group:

I go out every night, any time of the night, whenever I want to and come back whenever I want to and nobody does not bother me. Maybe I have a sign on me saying, Don't fuck with me! I don't know, but that is why I am telling you, I don't have no fear of nothing. Since I have been thirteen I have been on the street on my own . . . since I was thirteen. So now, I am used to it. If I am in the train, at five o'clock in the morning, it doesn't matter to me. I feel like it was the day.

I don't worry about nothing. That depends on what kind of attitude you have about outsiders. If you are a scary person and you act scared, act nervous, that is when attackers will always come, because they know. But if you act like, if you come over this way I am going to flip you, and they will not mess with you.

I am the same way. Let's say that I am sitting there, and I already know her attitude [pointing to another member of the group], if she is daring or is she not. You just look for the person's reaction.

By being on the streets, these three homeless teenagers report that they have learned how to "read" people's attitudes, as a way to protect themselves against fear. They are the "new witches," scapegoated but unafraid. Their "streetwise" attitude allows them to survive on the streets of New York City where their choices and opportunities are very limited.

Recent research on the social control of women focuses on their role as lawbreakers (Adler 1975; Faith 1993; Heidensohn 1985; Smart 1976). One set of studies maintains that women commit certain crimes as a result of social disadvantage. Typical women's crimes, such as shoplifting, credit card fraud, and writing bad checks, reflect women's economic powerlessness and serve as an extension of women's roles in society as consumers (Andersen 1993). Ironically, although women are expected to buy products, their powerless position limits their chances of consumption. Other typical female crimes, such as prostitution, are related to the commodification and objectification of women's bodies for male satisfaction. Women also turn to prostitution because they lack opportunities to obtain well-paying, decent jobs (Faith 1993).

A second set of studies emphasizes the dominant ideology within the different agencies of the criminal justice system when dealing with women's criminality. Ideas of femininity and of the proper behavior of a "good girl" permeate the police, the courts, and the correctional institutions. Even the term used by criminologists, "female offender," promotes "gender-based objectification and stereotyping" because it suggests that girls and women are "offensive in ways that men and boys are not and vice versa." The attachment of this label to women convicted of crimes denies the diversity of offenses committed by women, from murder to white collar crime, and stereotypes female criminals as "unruly girls" (Faith 1993, 57).

One of the major weaknesses in the study of social control has been the overemphasis on punishment and coercion. When one takes into consideration "the continuum of discipline from parents to school, the technologies of self-discipline, and the power of ideological representations, then prisons and police seem to occupy a more marginal, or at least more modest place in the maintenance of social order" (Platt 1994b, 74). In fact, most of the mechanisms that control women's lives can be found in the codes, symbols, words, rituals, and images transmitted and reinforced almost daily by the mass media, films, stories, and seemingly innocuous conversations between parents and children, teachers and students, coworkers and friends.

Although most of the research on the control of women focuses on lawbreaking, feminist researchers have more recently directed their attention toward other forces related to the control of women: their socioeconomic status and political powerlessness and the dominant narratives that constrain their lives. Pat Carlen (1994) presents an excellent summary of the principal areas of concern for these analysts. These areas include: the economy and the ideology of patriarchy; the discourse of femininity; the role of women within the family, and the welfare system.

Diverse studies examine the manner in which economics and the ideology of patriarchy are used to control women. James Messerschmidt (1986), for example, focuses on the influence of patriarchy and class relations in crime causation. He maintains that both class and gender relations play an important role in women's lawbreaking, by limiting women's opportunities for advancement. Other feminist writers maintain that both civil and criminal laws have a male "ethos." Catharine MacKinnon (1993) claims that the "state is male in the feminist sense." The state, she argues, "treats women the way men see and treat women." MacKinnon uses the example of rape laws to demonstrate the predominance of male views in the criminal law. The difference between rape and sex is seen as a matter of consent or women's will and the use of violence. However, women are socialized to be passive and submissive and men to be active and aggressive. In our society men control: they decide when, where, and how to have sex. Therefore, to prove lack of consent within a situation of inequality is a reflection of the male standpoint in the law.

Other studies seek to demonstrate how the prevailing "discourse of femininity"—the images of the feminine in popular narratives—helps to exert informal control of women. Several works have examined society's view of the "appropriate" role for women, its definitions of crime and deviance as they apply to women's lives, and its means of disciplining and policing girls' behaviors (Cain 1989). Karlene Faith (1993) explains how the voices of women who commit crimes are rarely heard sympathetically in Hollywood films. Indeed, when they are presented, female criminals are stereotyped as "masculinized monsters" (Faith 1993, 256). One example of this trend is the 1991 film *The Hand That Rocks the Cradle.* The image of a deceptive woman, played by Rebecca DeMornay, entrusted with the care of a child only to almost destroy a perfect family, fits the image of women criminals as possessed by evil forces. An earlier example of the same trend appears in *Fatal Attraction* (1987), where Glenn Close plays an obsessive, sick woman who gets in the way of a family that is seemingly happy except for the husband's "peccadilloes." Close's character exemplifies the image of the liberated/demonized woman who pays with her life at the hands of her lover's wife. Powerful women are frequently demonized and stereotyped as "masculine" and villainous in a similar way. As Frank Rich, the *New York Times* reviewer, asserts: "If a woman is going to be strong, she had better be the sexual predator of undying male fantasies, like Demi Moore in *Disclosure,* rather than the intellectually strong Jo March, who has the temerity to reject the hunk next door" (Faith 1993).

The work of Barbara Ehrenreich and Deirdre English (1978) clearly demonstrates the control that family and welfare institutions exert on women's lives. They argue that women's activities and opportunities have been limited by the definition of the home as the "woman's sphere" and as the refuge from the cold world of the marketplace, or public sphere. By relegating women to the home, society equates femininity with intuition and emotion and masculinity with rationality and competitiveness—and women's independence with the erosion of family values. In the field of social control, this dichotomy, which identifies the private sphere, or home, as "safe" for both men and women has created serious misunderstandings and misconceptions about women as victims of criminal behavior. Most people still associate crime with the public sphere. Recent studies on domestic violence, however, show that women have a higher chance of being victimized at home.

Social control theorist Carlen (1994) takes the study of the constraint of women into yet another direction by asking not why women break laws but why they conform to them. In most societies women commit much less crime than men. According to recent statistics, 11,765,764 persons were arrested by the police in 1994. Of those arrested, 80.5 percent were men and 19.5 percent were women (Bureau of Justice Statistics, 1995a, 386). According to FBI statistics, men are arrested more than women for every crime except prostitution and running away. Women are also detained less often than men. According to the 1991 Annual Survey of Jails, the average daily population for men was 381,458, and for women, 38,818—a ratio of ten men for each woman detained. The prison system reveals even more dramatic differences between men and women. In 1991 the country's state and federal facilities held 745,520 men and only 43,827 women—a rate of seventeen men for each woman (Bureau of Justice Statistics 1992, 590–608).

Although the number of women arrested is on the increase and the female population in the jails and prisons is also on the rise, the justice system still directs its repression predominantly toward men. One must then ask how society elicits compliance from women with less criminalization than men. Perhaps it is because the forms of social control imposed upon women are more restrictive and women's criminal behavior is considered more "deviant." While boys are expected to "raise hell," girls are taught to "behave" and to be "ladylike." Thus the control of women is primarily achieved through informal mechanisms—such as gender socialization and double standards of morality—making the use of master institutions of social control, such as the prison, less significant. As a feminist criminologist points out, the control of women may be "internal or external, implicit or explicit, private or public, ideological or repressive." Indeed, its "primary source" is to be found "outside or even beyond judicial influence" and, more precisely, within "seemingly innocuous social processes" (Smart and Smart 1978).

For Your Own Sake

One of the most significant mechanisms in the control of women's lives is the fear of crime. Its influence is masked by the common belief that fear of crime imposes limitations upon women's lives "for their own sake." As Elizabeth, a seventeen-year-old Latina, shared with the rest of the group during a lively discussion:

> I know, I know. I am not stupid. I know what you mean. I don't do many things that I would like to do. OK. That's true. But I know that when my boyfriend does not let me to go out after dark is because he cares about me and he wants to protect me. He is a man and he knows the streets better than I. There is a shitty world out there! Women are molested all the time. I am not going to go out at night just to show how tough I am.

One could rightly argue that Elizabeth's words reflect a crude reality: women are constant victims of harassment in the streets (Gardner 1995). The argument that I am advancing, though, is not that she should go out to "show how tough" she is. It is rather that the interaction between Elizabeth's boyfriend and herself reflects and sustains, at the microlevel of individual interaction, the gender breach that exists in society as a whole. He "knows the streets" and she should stay home where she will be safe. Elizabeth's "safety" is preserved in the name of love and care, without the use of billy clubs or a single move of the repressive apparatus.

Fear of crime is embedded in the prevailing "ideologies" or conceptions of crime that members of society share. These ideologies not only seek to explain the nature of crime, its causes, the way to control it, and how to avoid being victimized (Hall et al. 1978); they also contain a reservoir of images of criminals, victims, and the relations between them.

Two major conceptions, or ideologies, shape our images of crime and criminals in today's America. The more "conservative" view sees crime as the result of the deterioration of important social values—respectability, discipline, the work ethic, morality—all of which are represented and transmitted to us by a major social institution, the family. The way to control crime, according to the conservative view, is to restore these values through a more traditional family structure, and to control those who deviate with tougher laws, more police, and more prisons. The concept of family values has been at the forefront of Democratic and Republican agendas alike, with both parties competing to depict themselves as the ultimate moral crusaders (Becker 1964). According to the conservative view, criminals are undisciplined, they lack fundamental moral values, and many are unemployed, promiscuous, poor, and, of course, minorities. Conservatives believe that individuals and not social forces are to blame for the destruction of fundamental family values, yet they never address some of the systemic and historic roots of this erosion, for example, the split of extended and even nuclear families who are forced to relocate constantly in search of new jobs.

The "liberal" view of crime, on the other hand, blames forces outside the control of the individual such as failures in the socialization process, lack of education and opportunity, psychological problems, or all the above. According to the liberal view, criminals may be disturbed or psychotic individuals who go astray through no fault of their own or poor, undersocialized people who need to be brought back into the mainstream of society by re-education, job training, and the creation of role models to teach them how to be "good."

Of course, the liberal and conservative positions described here are only rough representations of the most common views of crime and criminals. We should not deny that a myriad of views depart from or in some way combine these two major conceptions. Nevertheless, they are particularly pertinent for the theme of this book because they are among the most commonly held views, and thus they offer us a general perspective on the public images of crime and criminals in the United States.

In the 1980s, the conservative view of crime began to secure better footing than the liberal view, becoming the dominant if not the only broadly acceptable approach. Several events precipitated the ascendance of this ideology. First, it is widely believed that today's social maladies arose from the permissive atmosphere of the 1960s and 1970s, and especially from the social movements that emerged during those times: the hippie movement, the antiwar movement, and the women's movement. For conservatives, these cultural phenomena are seen as leading causes of the destruction of fundamental values in American society. Speaker of the House Newt Gingrich claimed during one of the lectures in his now-famous televised college course that the beginning of American ills can be traced precisely to 1965 (Nelson 1995, A-8). Susan Faludi explains how during the Reagan/Bush era the women's movement and specifically feminism was blamed for different social maladies, from the destabilization of the family, to teenage suicide, to rising rates of crime (1991). "Liberated" women are presented as responsible for many of these social ills. In other words, if women would only go back to their homes, things would be different.

A second reason for the predominance of the conservative viewpoint has been the failure of the left to develop convincing counterarguments that provide a valid response to social problems affecting millions of Americans, such as teenage pregnancy, drugs, and neighborhood crime. The right has been very successful in linking a conservative view of crime to fundamental, traditional American values: self-discipline and self-reliance, work ethic, individual and civil responsibility, family and religious values, and respect for lawful authority. Moreover, conservatives have effectively connected the notion of being an American to these moral qualities. "Real Americans"—often considered only those of European descent—are decent, working, family-oriented, and disciplined people who respect authority and never break the laws (for a similar analysis of the sense of Englishness, see Hall et al. 1978, 138–177).

Crime is the negation of everything that conservative ideological representations associate with being an American. It is the denial of all these virtues: it is *anti-American,* as a bumper sticker that I recently saw proclaimed. Criminals are undisciplined, lazy, disrespectful, irresponsible, do not hold family and religious values, do not respect authority and break the laws. In a profoundly symbolic way, these conceptions transmit the idea that criminals are not real Americans, that they are a different breed. Moreover, to many the crime problem is a daily reminder of the failure of master social institutions such as the church, the school, and above all the family to inculcate these values, because it is especially within the family that they are passed on to the new generation. The popular discourse about the destruction of family values arouses public fears and anxieties because it touches themes that are fundamental to the American ethos. In this framework, crime—that is, street crime, not white collar crime—becomes a powerful organizing force because it gets to the "guts" of Americans.

I maintain that female fear is exacerbated by images and representations of crime contained in the prevailing ideology of crime (Hall et al. 1978). This ideology is shaped by dominant assumptions about what is criminal, who is more likely to commit a crime and who is more likely to become a victim, what the connections are between criminals and victims, where and when a crime is more likely to occur, and what the best ways are to control or prevent crime. These ideas reflect "attitudes so deeply embedded in tradition as to appear natural" (Reiman 1995, 6). By appealing to fundamental beliefs, these issues tend to rally Americans around politicians who vow to fight against crime and for "American values." In fact, these images are translated into a social ideology that cuts across class, race, and gender, creating a convincing, almost nationalized vision of crime and criminals. These images are held as valid by most members of our society regardless of their position in the various social hierarchies and regardless of their diverse and sometimes contradictory life experiences. They are incorporated into an uncodified, emotional, and enormously powerful ideological construct that is shared, at least to a certain extent, by almost everyone in our society (Hall et al. 1978). As Gramsci stated, the power of the

elites is based not only on the use of force, but above all on the ability
to control the intellectual and moral direction of a society and to provide models of "exemplary behavior" for its citizens (Pellicani 1981).

Liberal and conservative views overlap in one fundamental respect:
both see the family as the place where crime control must occur, while
the social structure in which the family exists remains immune from
criticism. Family values thus become the solution to many maladies,
especially crime, and the transmission of these values rests heavily on
the shoulders of women. The belief that women's primary responsibility is the care and protection of their children still prevails in most
of American society. Women are convinced that it is their fault if
something happens to their children, or if their children take the
"wrong path." This is not, by any means, only fantasy or delusion. Several recent court rulings unmistakably confirm the social reality of
these attitudes. A Washington judge recently denied a Senate aide
custody of her children because he deemed the mother more devoted
to her career than to the care of her offspring. A Michigan college
student also lost custody of her daughter because she put her in a
child care center to attend a good university (Chira 1994).

Feminist legal scholars claim that working mothers are penalized
because some judges consider career women "unmaternal" (Chira
1994). Women understand this and have internalized the feelings and
beliefs of their society. During a focus group, three African American
mothers express these fears unequivocally:

That's right. Because anything that happens with your child you always feel
it's your fault. There was something else you could have done. You are always
second-guessing yourself.

Usually I am home. So he [her sixteen-year-old son] expects from me to be
home every time. He has keys but he doesn't use them. He wants me to be
there. . . . I tell him to make sure that he takes his keys and this is every morning, and that I am always fearful that I won't be there sometimes he's left out
in the street. . . . Imagine if something happens to him or if he gets in trouble. So I always stay home waiting for him.

Mom's always there. I am always there, most of the time. If I am not I am on
my way.

Yes, the reality is that the safety of the children depends on women.

Women who have to leave their children in child care centers feel "as if we were doing something wrong." Many mothers feel scared by reports that child care centers are flawed (Quindlen 1994). A recent book by Penelope Leach, the British, so-called child care guru has given women more reasons to worry and to feel guilty if they have to work. Leach claims that "unless society allows children more time with their parents in the early years, when IQ, temperament, values and a child's chances for success are largely determined . . . babies harmed by part-time parenting will cost society more than it can af-ford later: Violence, crime, drug addiction, all the main problems of Western post-industrial societies" (Kinkead 1994).

As the African American women expressed during the focus group, however, full-time parenting often means full-time mothering, since women are still more likely to stay home than men. In addition, rather than providing more money for child care centers, government subsidies in this area are being curtailed. Women's options are therefore much more limited for fear that if something happens to the children "it is going to be my fault."

The reality is that most women work because they have to. Most families cannot afford to live with only one salary. Moreover, the United States has the highest rate of divorce of any country in the world: for every two marriages in one year, there is one divorce. In other words, 50 percent of the marriages today end in divorce (U.S. Bureau of Census 1990). Furthermore, increasing numbers of homes are headed by single women, especially by women of color (Sidel 1992). But even in two-parent families, women are still the primary caregivers of the children and the primary guardians of family values.

Many images associated with women as guardians of family values have traditionally been used as a means of social control. For example, Barbara Ehrenreich and Deirdre English (1978) explain how twentieth-century psychology has helped to develop the figure of the "bad mother" by portraying maternal deprivation as one of the major causes of children's psychological and behavioral problems. Quoting from John Bowlby's book, *Maternal Care and Mental Health,* Ehrenreich and English explain how family failure has been attributed to factors ranging from "death of a parent" to "full employment of the mother." Thus a major fear is placed in a mother's mind: if she fails, her children may become drug addicts or even criminals. Women are the ones that have to be home to be sure that their children become "responsible citizens," don't get involved in drugs, and don't get into trouble. The message is: be a good mother; stay home or your family will fail, and it will be your fault. Thus the fear of crime reinforces gender roles within the family, with women seen as the primary care-takers and guardians of the children and their safety.

Women's fear about the possible victimization of their children or about their possible involvement in deviant or criminal behaviors has political consequences. It induces social conformity by corralling women within the parameters of rigid gender expectations, perpetu-ating gendered relations not only at home but also in different do-mains of social life: work and public space. Women, more often than men, have to limit their activities so they can be "good mothers" and protect their children by driving or walking them to school, picking them up, helping with their homework. All these activities place lim-its upon the educational level women can achieve, the type of work they can get, and the nature of their work schedules. In addition, as we have said, women bear an enormous share of the responsibility in the control of crime. Because women need to take care of themselves, they don't go to the "wrong places" (like the Central Park jogger), do the "wrong things" (like Carol Ann Artutis, the woman whose body was discovered in a trailer in New York City), wear the "wrong clothes," or interact in the "wrong way" with the "wrong people." But they also have to protect their children so they do not become "bad." Thus women, in most instances, do not need the police, the courts, the prisons to be controlled, because their control is informal and in-ternalized, but no less insidious and constraining.

Fear of crime is indeed an extremely dominant force in the control of women's lives. Images of crime, criminals, victims, and the rela-tionships among them help to organize public consent around issues such as what places are safe for women to be in and at what times, what behaviors are appropriate for women and what for men, and what roles are proper for males and what for females.

Josepha, a thirty-year-old, white middle-class woman who lives in the suburbs of New York City, shared the following narrative with me:

You know, I hadn't thought about it before. Now that we are having this conversation. . . . Hmmm! I realize how many things I do not do because of my fears. . . . What makes me angry is that I do it so natural. You know . . . like if it is the normal thing to do. I just don't do them. Nobody tells me that I don't have to do them. But, I know, somehow that if I do them, like going to a bar by myself, or even to a restaurant or . . . even to the movies or for a walk at night . . . even around here, which is supposed to be safe . . . I may be in trouble and then everybody will say: Is she nuts or what? So, I just don't do them. I ask my boyfriend to come with me.

From birth, invisible walls are built around women, limiting their lives and activities. The strict rules of conduct imposed upon women under the flag of "keeping them safe" make the need for formal control agencies less significant. Consequently, the study of the social constraints on women must take into account the fear of crime. Such a study should be conducted outside the context of traditional criminological theories of crime and punishment. Rather it should examine the material, everyday conditions of women's lives, using forms of language and communication that facilitate the sharing and understanding of women's diverse experiences, according to their age, race, socioeconomic class, and sexual orientation.

Current ideologies of crime are filled with representations of women as victims of crimes and men as offenders; with images of who is a criminal, who is a victim, and where, when, and why a crime is likely to occur. Women are constantly forced to forgo activities that are enjoyable to them, such as taking a walk during a summer night, going to a public park by themselves, or, as Josepha says, even going to a movie or to a restaurant. The fear that "something bad can happen to them" teaches women at a very early age what "their place" is; who is expected to be strong and who weak; who should be protected and who should protect; what type of clothes women should wear and what type of activities they should or should not engage in. If these clear, gendered rules of behavior are not strictly followed, women get the blame for their own victimization, because good women are supposed to "know better."

Chapter Three

Fear of Crime as Social Control

The possibility of being the victim of a crime is ever present on my mind; thinking about it is as natural as . . . breathing. . . .The most unsettling crime is that of being cornered and attacked by a group of youths while riding in an empty train car and being violently hurt. . . . There is no place to run, no help available, and being at the mercy of this pack of animals.

Michaela, a forty-year-old middle-class
white woman who lives in upper Manhattan, New York

Although many researchers have studied the fear of crime, few have attempted to define it. As Mark Warr (1984) observes, the phrase *fear of crime* has been used to define so many different feelings, emotions, and attitudes that it has lost its specificity. Most authors avoid defining the concept and instead choose one or more questions that they believe will elicit information about fear of crime from respondents (Ferraro and LaGrange 1987; LaGrange and Ferraro 1989). Two of the most common questions are, "How safe would you feel being out alone in your neighborhood during the day and night?" (Balkin 1979; Box et al. 1988; Covington and Taylor 1991; Garofalo 1979; Liska et al. 1991; Maxfield 1984; Taylor and Covington 1993) and, "Is there any area right around here—that is, within a mile—where you would be afraid to walk alone at night?" (Braungart et al. 1980; Clemente and Kleiman 1977; Ortega and Myles 1987). Other authors ask respondents more specific questions, such as how afraid they are about becoming a victim of specific crimes or whether they worry about family members (LaGrange and Ferraro 1989; Taylor and Hale 1986; Warr 1984; Warr and Stafford 1983). These two types of questions measure different social facts. The first category measures the willingness of individuals to risk walking around their neighborhood alone during the night or day, whereas the latter category concerns the emotions that the possibility of victimization elicits in respondents.

Webster's New American Dictionary defines fear as "an unpleasant, often strong emotion caused by expectation or awareness of danger." When people experience fear of crime, they have the expectation or awareness of a very specific danger, the danger of becoming the victim of a criminal act. To know whether a person is afraid of crime, therefore, we need to know at least the following information: First, does the possibility of victimization elicit any emotion in the respondent? What type of emotion is this? Is it concern, worry, awareness, preoccupation, disquietude, apprehension, panic, terror? Do these emotions reflect different dimensions or levels of fear? Second, does the person expect something to happen to her? Does she link specific crimes and images to these expectations? What are these images? An important related question often used in studies on fear of crime asks, Are these images influenced by a sense of vulnerability or by gender, race, or socioeconomic background? The answers to these questions should offer information that will help us conceptualize and understand the fear of crime.

Given the differences in their socialization, men and women may differ greatly regardless of their race or class in their willingness to acknowledge that they are afraid and in their disposition to risk victimization. Their answers may therefore not reflect their actual feelings. The methodological implications of these differences in studies of fear of crime are major and have received surprisingly scant attention. Most studies show that women are more afraid of crime than men; these findings may, however, be tainted by the fact that women, by virtue of their socialization, are more open to admitting their fears or to acknowledge their unwillingness to put themselves at risk. Moreover, women may possess a greater awareness of their vulnerability to violence because of their socially disadvantaged position (Stanko 1990, 14–15).

Similar methodological problems may also arise in studies of individuals from different age groups, since young people may also be less likely to acknowledge their fears and, as some studies show, more likely to take risks than older people (Gove 1985). Unwillingness to express fear and willingness to take risks do not, however, mean that a respondent is less afraid. Therefore, it becomes a methodological challenge to elicit valid responses from people of different age groups about their feelings of fear. This issue may also be relevant when dealing with people from different cultural and ethnic backgrounds, since some either express their feelings more freely than others or convey those feelings in different ways. Similarly, class background and education may also influence the expression of one's sentiments. For example, people in the higher classes and more educated people might select their words more carefully or may voice their feelings in a less emotional manner.

I chose to deal with the methodological challenges of studying fear of crime among women from different age, class, and racial backgrounds by framing the topic with a very general question, such as, "Do you think that crime is a problem in your city/town?" "In your neighborhood?" I then followed up with more specific questions: "Have you thought about the possibility of becoming the victim of a crime?" "What about someone you know: friends, family members?" Then I asked, "How would you describe those feelings?" "What would *you* call them?" I found this approach to be interesting because it gave participants the opportunity to voice their feelings in their own words, not those of the interviewer.

Worried, Concerned, Afraid, or Just Mad?

Although statistics show that teenagers and young adults consistently have the highest victimization rates (Bureau of Justice Statistics 1996), very few studies have focused on the fear of crime among teenagers. For this research, seven of the focus groups were carried out with teenage Latina, Black, and white women in New York City and in the suburbs of New York and northern New Jersey.

These teenagers described their feelings in a myriad of words and expressions. For example, here is how a group of Puerto Rican teenagers in a Latino neighborhood in upper Manhattan expressed their feelings:

The word I use is scared.

I get angry. I don't know why . . . but I get angry.

I fear for myself and other people I care for.

I worry about the little kids.

I don't know, I have never had to explain how I feel. I just feel afraid.

I call them experience, because you see what is out there, so when you see what is out there then you are like that. This is why my mother is scared, because she has experience.

One of the group participants, Rosa, who is fifteen years old, expressed several different emotions at once:

I get mad, mad, mad. Because every time you get to step out of your house, you got to fear. My problem is that I worry, because I got to worry about what is going to happen. I am always thinking, damn, what if it happens? I am always trying to prepare myself, what if this happens, what if this happens to my family. I worry more than I fear, because I know it is going to happen, as much as I worry about it and find out what I would do if it happens.

These Latina teenagers express their feelings in different ways. They are afraid, scared, angry, mad, worried, or even "experienced." This last expression reflects the reality in which some of these teenagers live. Many of them have been victims of crimes or have witnessed crimes at a very early age. Rosa, for example, expresses the frustration of living in a high-crime area and facing the possibility of being a victim of a crime every time "you get to step out of your house." Her words reveal the expectation—as the Webster's definition states—that something is going to happen to her or to her family. But instead of naming a specific crime, Rosa says that she knows "it" will eventually happen. She is therefore always trying to prepare herself. When questioned about what that "it" might be, Rosa explains, "You know, that one person in my family can get hurt or . . . I am even afraid to say it . . . killed."

Sitting on the floor of the living room in a middle class home in the suburbs of northern New Jersey, a group of Latina teenagers, ages fifteen and sixteen, shared their feelings about the possibility of being victims of a crime. When questioned about their choice of a word to express those feelings, one of them, Rosario, gave a revealing answer:

I think it is more fear than anything. Worrying is only part of it, because you are worried and concerned, you think about it all the time and then you become scared.

In other words, Rosario believes that her fear is the result of worrying about it all the time. These worries and concerns lead her to become scared.

Margaret, a fourteen-year-old white teenager who grew up in Manhattan and now lives in Brooklyn, reveals during the interview that she used to worry. But now, she says, "I don't think that things are going to happen. Now I am aware." By being "aware" Margaret means, "I just look around." She comments that sometimes, especially during the night, the thought crosses her mind that something could happen. But, she says, "it is not that I am, OH MY GOD! I AM SCARED!" (raising her voice and using a high pitch, imitating a little girl's voice). In other words, Margaret makes a distinction between being aware of her surroundings and being fearful.

Some people have moved to the suburbs to "escape" crime and the reactions it produces, just to find out that crime also exists in their new surroundings. In a group interview with six teenagers in a predominantly white, working-class small town in northern New Jersey, a fourteen-year-old woman talks about being "always afraid" and about her mother's feelings after moving to the suburbs:

She was a New Yorker and we moved here. We never thought that all this was happening here. We also live in fear here.

In contrast, a group of six African American teenagers in a middle-class, racially mixed town in northern New Jersey expressed their lack of fear:

I am not afraid on the streets of this town. It is safe compared with other places.

I don't feel in danger at all.

I walk where I want, and I just don't think about it.

Claudia, one of the participants in the group, remarked:

I really believe that the real danger for women is more inside of our homes and in our schools.

Of all the teenagers interviewed, Claudia was the only one who recognized the fact that women are more likely to be victimized at home than in the streets. Claudia believes that women should be more afraid of people they know. "You are more likely to be raped by a friend. I always think twice before I go out with a boy," she concluded. Latina and white teenagers were more ready than Blacks to admit that they were afraid, scared, worried, even mad. Although some of them live in areas considered unsafe, others live in suburban neighborhoods with lower crime rates. But the African American teenagers, including some who endure the most difficult circumstances because they are homeless, did not reveal the same feelings. According to criminal statistics, young Black girls are the second most likely group to be victims of crime (Bureau of Justice Statistics 1996). However, some of the African American teenagers confirm that although on some occasions fear of crime may be quite realistic, on other occasions they are able to develop a sense of "street smartness" or an attitude that protects them against fear (Stanko 1990). These young women may be reluctant to express their fears because they need to show toughness to survive on the streets. "I don't fear nothing" was a more common expression among African American teenagers than among whites or Latinas.

Different Words or Different Worlds?

Adult women also expressed their sentiments in various ways. A group of ten Spanish-speaking Latina women, some of them undocumented, who attended an English as a Second Language program in upper Manhattan chose the following words and phrases to express their feelings: "that is my daily *preocupación* (preoccupation)." "It is a constant, constant *preocupación*." "And also *temor* (fear)," claimed another participant. "I feel *coraje* (rage)." One is never *tranquila* (tranquil)." "I feel *insegura* (unsafe) everywhere and at any time." "I am always *nerviosa* (nervous)." "I live in constant *zozobra* (anxiety)." "I am *desesperada* (desperate)." These expressions highlight not only the different concepts and words the women used to describe their feelings but also the fact that several women said that these feelings are a constant, daily preoccupation for them. Whatever their feelings—preoccupation, unsafety, anger, anxiety, nervousness—these adult Latinas reported that they feel them everywhere, and all the time. When asked about the word she would use to express her emotions,

one of the participants burst into tears. After sobbing for some min-
utes she said, "I am so preoccupied and it gives me so much anger, to
have to live this way." Other participants expressed similar feelings of
anger at having to live with this constant preoccupation. One forty-
year-old Latina claimed: "Yes, I am in panic, in great panic, it makes
me very nervous."

Pilar, a twenty-eight-year-old African American woman, said, "I am
not just afraid. I am actually paranoid." Of the twenty-eight African
American adult and senior women interviewed, only a handful said
that they were not afraid. The rest expressed their fears in different
ways: "I feel threatened," one woman claimed. At a senior program in
the Lower East Side of Manhattan, two elderly African American
women expressed their different feelings about crime. Bell stated that
"I am alert, not afraid," whereas Sylvia said that she does not feel
afraid: "I don't worry about it. What is going to happen is going to
happen."

In the apartment of one of my Hunter college students in the
Upper East Side of Manhattan, a group of middle-class white women
discussed the issue in a very lively way:

Of course, crime affects me and my family. . . . I always think, well, if something happens to me, how will this affect my family?

I wouldn't say that is fear. I feel more alert. But I don't feel fearful. . . . I
think more like prevention. I don't feel fearful, but I think that in New York
City you must be on the alert and not take things for granted, but I don't feel
fearful.

I feel something very alert, but not fearful.

I am more on guard than worried.

I didn't notice my apprehension until last year, when I went to Vancouver,
Canada, where I felt much safer. . . . When I am in New York I have a constant feeling of apprehension that I do not even recognize within myself, because being on guard is almost normal for me.

You have to be cautious, that's all . . . and exercise your judgment.

I have a lot of anger, because crime is a reality and because I am always apprehensive. . . . I am kind of angry when I look to those other countries that
do not have these problems.

Clearly, reactions to crime, or more precisely to the possibilities of victimization, are diverse. These findings reveal, as some authors have stated, that "fear of crime" actually comprises various emotional, subjective, and in many cases objective appraisals of a situation (DuBow et al. 1979). When people are given the opportunity to express their sentiments in their own words, a complex picture begins to emerge. Table 1 presents the types of reactions given by the participants. First are reactions to the possibility of victimization, which reveal various magnitudes of emotion, from apprehension to panic or desperation, from anger to rage. Such sentiments are not clearly reflected in the commonly used phrase "fear of crime." Second are the reactions of middle-class adult white women who chose words such as "on the alert," "on guard," or "aware" more often than some of the Latino and African American women. The third type of reaction either assesses a situation as unsafe or reveals the expectation that a crime is likely to occur. Only the first of these categories involves the sorts of emotional reactions implied by the phrase "fear of crime." All categories, however, express reactions to the possibility of victimization. Clearly, these reactions are more complex than many of the studies on fear of crime imply. In fact, as one of the participants pointed out, one category of reaction may lead to another, creating an intricate web of emotions, attitudes, and assessments.

TABLE 1.   Reactions to Crime

Emotions	*Attitudes*	*Assessments*
panic, desperation	guardedness	unsafe
fear	alertness	dangerous
worry	awareness	threatening
nervousness	prevention	risky
preoccupation	caution	
apprehension		
concern		
fearlessness		
anger, rage		

Previous studies that have examined the fear of crime have neglected to ask why it is that some people are *not* afraid. The attitude of acceptance expressed by some of the teenagers interviewed in this study is especially startling. During the focus groups and in-depth interviews they conveyed a fatalistic view. Clara, a homeless Black teenager, provides a good example of this tendency:

You know that something will happen. It will be that way. No matter what you do, it will happen. So, why would you fear something that you know that there is nothing you can do to stop that from happening to you? So, why would you be scared? It is nonsense.

There is in fact a very high probability that a homeless teenager on the streets of a large city will become a crime victim. Although some react with fear, others, like Clara, feel that if something is going to happen, there is nothing they can do about it. These words clearly reflect the lack of control that Clara perceives in her life and the circumstances surrounding it. One of the few controls Clara has, she exercises: control over her own feelings. One is left with the impression that Clara and others like her have crossed a threshold beyond which fear ceases to exist. Fear has a positive side to it: it helps to preserve one's life and protect against victimization. But in extremely harsh social conditions where protection is impossible, as in the case of this homeless teenager, the fear seems to cease and is transformed into acceptance or fatalism.

A Position of Fear

Women experience emotional, attitudinal, or assessive reactions to the possibility of victimization both of themselves and of others (family members, friends). During the last twenty years, however, studies on fear of crime have focused almost exclusively on the fear of personal victimization and neglected what is known as "altruistic fear" (Warr 1992). Among the 140 women interviewed for this book, however, practically all of those with children said that they worry not just about themselves but *primarily* about their sons and daughters. Others worry about their husbands, friends, sisters, grandmothers, or cousins.

More than half of the participants in the study said they were more afraid for others than for themselves. Many used phrases such as "I don't worry about myself, but I worry about my family." For example, Ivette, one of the homeless African American teenagers, said: "I don't fear nothing, but I am afraid for my little baby." These fears were evident among all the women that had children. African American women were particularly afraid for their sons. Several Black mothers who live in the Bronx revealed their deep preoccupations in a somber tone of voice:

My biggest fear is when my son makes eighteen . . . walking around here.

Me too. He is big and six-two and two hundred something. He is a threat just looking at him, because he is Black and big. He is a threat to people and he also is a threat to the cops.

Because he is so big, all he has to do is put his hands in his pocket and say something smart. The cops'll shoot him.

After a discussion of the dangers that drugs and HIV pose for their children, Sue, one of the participants, claimed:

I really worry about drugs. You know, they are so young. They could get involved. I mean, some of them are involved. The things that they have to deal with as teenagers we never had to deal with.

These feelings are not limited to African American mothers. Angela and Patricia, two single, young adult African American women with no children, echoed the feelings of the concerned mothers:

I worry a lot about my male cousin. . . . You know, the rate of crime is more in adolescent Afro-American males; they are the number one target. I mean, mostly it's the Black young men that are dying out. . . . I mean, I don't worry too much about the females. But I worry more about the males.

I worry about my brothers because they wear expensive clothes and jewelry. I worry about them going on the train with expensive clothes and jewelry.

I then asked Patricia, "But what about the concern that something may happen to you?" She responded, "I worry more about my brothers, you know." African American women worry about their sons, brothers, cousins, fathers, and uncles because their rate of violent victimization is extremely high: 63 per 1,000 persons. In comparison, the rate of victimization among white males is 36 per 1,000, or 42 percent lower than that among Black males (Bureau of Justice Statistics

1994b). In addition, these women also express the fear that their male relatives may be victims of police brutality. This fear was never mentioned by the white mothers interviewed in this study.

The fears of Latina mothers, especially those living in urban areas, were similar to those of African American women. Maria, a single, forty-year-old Latina mother of two teenagers who lives in a neighborhood in Brooklyn that she describes as "drug ridden," expressed her feelings in this way:

I live in constant fear because of my children. I constantly ask God to help me to leave the place where we live. I want to leave New York and move somewhere else. I moved here fifteen years ago and the place was safe. Now there is drugs. Many men on the street selling drugs. I live in great panic. It makes me so nervous that I have to take medicines.

A thirty-two-year-old Latina woman, Mireya, who lives in a predominantly Latino neighborhood in upper Manhattan, reported that she does not sleep during the night until her husband and her two sons return from work. "They work a lot," she said, and when they come home late, "I have images of them dead, bleeding, laying on the streets." White mothers also expressed fear for their children. In contrast to the African American mothers, however, they claim to be more afraid for their daughters than for their sons. During a group discussion, Marianne, thirty-six, an Anglo mother of a nine-year-old daughter, expressed the way she feels:

I worry a lot about my daughter. My daughter is now traveling all by herself on a public bus. . . . She is very large, but still I worry a lot about that.

Eve, another participant in the same group discussion, added that "women are more protective than men are, in terms of someone doing something to the children." Other respondents had similar comments: "The more things change, the more they remain the same," "Children are still women's responsibility," and "The buck stops at women."

Childlessness, however, is no safeguard against fear. African American and Latina women who do not have children worry more than white women about their male acquaintances and relatives: brothers, cousins, fathers. Latina and white teenagers and young adults also shared concerns about female relatives: their mothers, grandmothers, sisters. Heather, a twenty-two-year-old white woman who goes to college in a small town in upstate New York, worries a lot about her mother, a career woman who travels around the country on business, because "sometimes the office that she is working in is not in the best part of town." Sandra, another participant in the same discussion group feared for her niece and her nephew. Her major worry was that "they will be kidnapped." She continued,

I go to the store always watching and keeping an eye on my niece because . . . some people, they have lost their child.

Contrary to the public perception, more children are kidnapped by a family member than by a stranger; nevertheless, several women expressed fear of stranger abductions. Marcia, a Latina, said she was afraid to go out with her children, because she had heard that a woman's children were kidnapped when she suffered a dizzy spell.

Fear of Crime and Social Vulnerability

Some studies relate fear of crime to the social vulnerability of women (Skogan and Maxfield 1981). But are all women equally vulnerable? Do particular situations make some women more vulnerable than others? In this study, immigrant women, undocumented women, and those who did not speak English expressed a particular sense of vulnerability and helplessness. Several immigrant, Spanish–speaking women who attend an English as a Second Language class expressed their feelings of helplessness in a very clear way. Leida, a twenty-four-year-old woman who lives in the Bronx, said:

Here, they treat Hispanic people very badly. . . . If you don't speak English they treat you like if you are nobody. There is a lot of discrimination.

[The rest of the group said at once]

Muchísima . . . (a whole lot).

Yes, they see us as inferior.

It has to do with race.

And with language.

And the culture too; we have a different culture.

And with the fact that we are women.

"How would you feel if you could speak English?" I asked them. "I would feel much safer," answered one. "At least I could call the police." "Yes," another responded,

> One day I called the police because I was molested by a man on the streets. I asked if there was someone who could speak Spanish. The person who took the telephone told me, "If you cannot speak English why don't you go back to your country? Call us when you learn English."

Aura, a sixteen-year-old Puerto Rican who participated in one of the focus groups and lives in a Latino neighborhood in Brooklyn, expressed similar feelings:

> Like my mother said, you are born with two strikes already: you are Puerto Rican and you are a woman. So, if something happens to you, nobody is going to help. I think it's worse for us Latinas, because we are in the middle, between Black and white . . . so it is like, we get it from both ways, you know? So, a Black may get mad because we have a nice tan or a white may get mad because we speak Spanish. . . . So we got the worst of it.

During recent decades, researchers have referred to "female fear of crime" as if it were the same feeling for most women, and it is not. Women's concerns, worries, and fears are neither identical nor irrational; rather they are linked to the position that an individual occupies in the social structure: socioeconomic class, role, age, race (Sparks 1982, 33), and even immigrant status. Thus the fears and the images that shape the feelings of a teenager in the suburbs are different from the fears of a single African American mother who lives in "the projects" or public housing and from the fears of an undocumented immigrant woman who does not speak English and does not have a social support network.

Older women, for example, are particularly afraid of being assaulted or mugged when going to the bank. As a white woman in her late seventies emphatically claimed during the group interview in a program for senior citizens: "I am afraid for myself. Not for anybody else. I already had my social security check stolen." White and Black women differ as well. Unlike Black women, white women rarely report concern about a male relative, and even when they did, their worries were unrelated to police brutality. Indeed, in the few instances when white women reported fear for the men in their lives, their feelings were linked to the fact that the men worked in a "bad area of the city," had previously been victims of a crime, or had adopted "this macho attitude, you know, and they can be killed."

Many white women worry about children in general, especially about their daughters and the violence that they face in the schools today. Others, like Judith, worry about other female members of the family: "I worry about my mother," she said, "but at least she has my dad over her shoulder." In other words, her worries about her mother are somewhat allayed because there is a man, her father, protecting her. Some women's fears are less specific. Nancy, a thirty-five-year-old white woman, is very sensitive toward her body and her use of space. "If someone comes too close to me, I feel like putting my fist in his face, you know."

Mothers' and fathers' fears limit children's lives and impose rules and regulations upon them to keep them safe. It is impossible to estimate the psychological effect of this "hypervigilance" on children. Girls especially are warned against sexual molestation, against talking to strangers, even against "Uncle John's pats." Children are exposed to a multitude of news, from a mother drowning her sons in a lake to strangers kidnapping girls from their own rooms. "I have taught my little brother to jump inside of the bathtub when we hear gun shots," one of my students recently shared with me. "I don't like my daughter near the window," another of my interviewees said. "She can be hit by a stray bullet." Although the impact of fear of crime on children is not the subject of this book, it is an area of research in need of much attention (Adler 1994, 43–49).

The group of white working-class teenagers expressed concerns about the situation in their suburban schools:

There is stuff going on around in school; there are a lot of fights, and this year alone, stuff has been stolen from me. Just coming home from school today I heard about a big fight and all the cops were there.

I am really afraid of theft, definitely. I had something in the locker. They already took my leather jacket, and one time last year they stole earrings from me and they stole money from me.

In a neighboring town also in suburban northern New Jersey, a group of middle-class African American high school students also expressed their feelings about fights in their schools.

In our school, you walk down the hallway and they look at you the wrong way or you look at them the wrong way and you know what happen.

What happens?

They'd say: What are you looking at? And instigate conflict. Like that girl. For no reason at all.

Mothers living in New York City were also alarmed by the situation in the schools. Gisela, a twenty-five-year-old Latina who lives in a predominantly Latino and Black neighborhood on the Upper East Side of Manhattan, mentioned that she had to take her son out of school because of the fear that he could be hurt or even killed. "He was the best student of the school," she said, and "the rest of the students hated him." According to Gisela's story, one day, after classes were over, a group of boys waited for her son outside school. The principal became aware of the situation and protected the boy by walking him to his home. After that incident Gisela was so afraid of what could happen to her child that she removed him from the school. "I do not mind if he misses one year. Better than being killed," she concluded.

What about You?

It was not until late in our discussions that most women felt encouraged to talk about the possibility of their own victimization. Even when they were reporting the fears about themselves, they often expressed them in the terms of, "If something happens to me, how is this going to affect my family?"

Although the literature on women's fear of crime focuses primarily on rape, this research shows a wide gamut of emotions regarding different crimes, often linked to the objective reality of the individual woman. For example, Maria, a Latina who had been mugged at knifepoint in the subway, observed that her major fear is "to be cut" (with a knife). Patricia, a twenty-two-year-old African American woman who lives in a predominantly Black, lower-class area in Brooklyn, says:

I am very worried about gun problems. It is like, you know, Black on Black crime; it is very hard in my neighborhood. Anything, any kind of dispute in my neighborhood, a gun is involved as the solution. And that worries me because it is not only consequences for two guys fighting and they are shooting or whatever, I may be passing from nowhere and I get a stray bullet.

In fact, Patricia said that her major fear was robbery, not rape:

Robbery, I really don't think about rape. . . . Because I live in the projects and, you know . . . it is the thing that happens a lot. Most of the time where I live the crime is robbery, stealing and pocketbook snatching . . . robbing girls for jewelry.

Ten of the Black women in the study mentioned their fear of hate crime. Lily and Marianne, two African American women in their twenties, expressed this fear:

I live in Bensonhurst, and there is a lot of racial tension in that area. You know the Yusuf Hawkins case [a Black teenager who was killed by a group of white teenagers]. I grew up there. White people and Black people are always fighting. You are hesitant to walk into the so-called white area after dark. If you walk over there and try to go to the store or something, they call you nigger.

When we were little I went to the elementary school in the area. We had a sniper who use to shoot at the Black students. And then, during and after the Yusuf Hawkins case, I was in my first year of high school. . . . Some of the white kids I went to school with, they were against the line calling us niggers and telling us to get out of their neighborhood. . . . They used to chase us from school.

Three African American teenagers living in the suburbs of northern New Jersey revealed similar feelings. They said they were especially worried now that they were in their junior year. "Next year we have to decide what school to go to," Betsy said. "And I am afraid because I have heard of so many racial incidents going on in college campuses."

White women, particularly young adult women, were more likely than Black or Latina women to express the fear of rape. Judith, a twenty-one-year-old middle-class white woman, reported being particularly afraid of rape by someone "breaking into the house or something, who will tie you up and rape and abuse you. . . ." Nancy, a thirty-year-old white woman, said that sometimes she felt afraid of being raped by someone following her, grabbing her, and pushing her into a car. Other women were also fearful that their daughters could be kidnapped and raped.

Why is it that the white women interviewed in this study reported being more concerned about rape than Black and Latina women? One plausible explanation is that the media tend to portray white women as victims of rape more often than Black or Latina women. Several recent cases of rape reported by the media, such as the Central Park jogger or the Greenwich Village victim whose body was found in a trailer, illustrate this important fact. Josephine, a twenty-three-year-old white woman, actually said to me:

Just look at the newspaper; who are more likely to be raped? . . . I do not know if this is true or not, and it doesn't matter. It *seems that way* when you read the newspaper [italics added].

Josephine is right. Where fear of crime is concerned, what is more important than the actual statistics is our images of crime. These images are greatly influenced by the stories we hear from other people. They are also affected by the manner in which crime is presented and interpreted by the media, who benefit from our anxieties by increasing their newspaper sales and program ratings, and by politicians, who sensationalize certain crimes in order to promote their political agendas.

All the women who mentioned rape as their major concern feared being victims of strangers following them, breaking into their houses, lurking in the dark. These images are consistent with the prevalent ideologies of crime as presented by the media and politicians. Very few of the participants said they were afraid of being raped by their friends, boyfriends, or colleagues, who are the more likely aggressors. As I will discuss later, it is only in two special settings that women expressed fear of someone they knew: (1) several respondents said they were afraid of being sexually harassed by a coworker or a teacher; (2) a few respondents claimed to be afraid of becoming victims of domestic violence by their partners.

Participants in this study reported being victims of various crimes: burglary; purse snatching; pickpocketing; personal assault; sexual harassment at work, in school, and in the streets; mugging; rape; domestic violence; and the murder of a family member. The phrase "violence against women" normally refers to crimes such as sexual assault, domestic violence, rape, and other types of sex-related crimes. Yet many other crimes are committed against women simply because they are women. Two examples illustrate this point. Maria, a Latina woman, recounted:

I have been assaulted several times. Once a man hit me in the eye with his fist and he also pulled my hair. I was leaving the train when this man pulled my hair and then he held me. When I was turning around, he took my purse.

Maria never reported this crime to the police: "What are they going to do? Nothing!" she claimed. This type of crime, however, was committed against Maria because she is a woman. Just imagine an offender pulling a man's hair—it does not happen. Furthermore, purse snatching is a very frequent crime against women in New York City. Some women are dragged, and some have been killed by cars while an aggressor is pulling on their purses. A large number of purse snatchings, however, are never reported to the police. Angela, a twenty-three-year-old African American student, reported another such victimization:

I have been a victim of a crime three times. Exactly now is about two years ago. I live next to this beauty parlor where I go there occasionally. . . . I went to the store to purchase some beverages and when I came back there were four guys outside. . . . One of the guys came behind me with a gun. . . . I told the owner of the beauty parlor: if you don't let me in I will get shot. So she had to let me in. They took all my jewelry, my $495 watch, and my diamond ring that my boyfriend at the time had bought me.

Robberies around beauty parlors have become frequent in New York and New Jersey. Because women often go to these places to relax and have some time away from home, beauty parlors are seen as "easy targets" for robbers. Another example of a crime committed against a woman was that of Beth, a twenty-seven-year-old African American woman who reported having been hit by a taxi driver, over "one dollar and fifty cents." "I got bumped in my face" she said. Of course, "he thought that he could get away with it because I am a woman," she concluded.

Eight participants reported being burglarized. Others reported being in the midst of a shootout and being robbed at gunpoint. Three also reported that their children had been robbed at gunpoint. One Latina woman saw her brother being killed. Another was called by the police to identify her brother's body, which was found in a plastic bag. Although it is true that men are more likely to be the victims of murder, women have to live with the horror and trauma that accompanies it for the rest of their lives. "Every time I go out and I see the black trash bags, I feel a profound pain." These women were called to testify, to identify the bodies of their brothers. They were the ones who had to inform their families. In addition, they felt the moral responsibility of "holding the family together." One of them has been on antidepressants since her brother was killed. "That's the only way I can get out of bed," she said to me. Thus, in more than one way, these women were also victims of the murders.

Some places that seem to be especially frightening to women are those that limit the possibility of escape: trains, elevators, building entrances or hallways, and parking lots and garages were frequently mentioned. An empty street or a street or school hallway crowded with a group of male teenagers were also considered frightening situations:

I freak when I walk down the street and I see a group of men walking toward me.

Or when there is someone following you.

My agony is the elevators.

Several of the women also said that they were afraid to enter their cars without checking the back seat. "Someone can be hiding there," said eighteen-year-old Kay. Having just received her driver's license and enjoying her relative freedom, she said it was "a drag to have to worry about things like that."

Sexual Harassment and Fear of Crime

One topic that has been largely neglected in the literature is the connection between fear of crime in general and the crimes and acts of aggression typically committed against women, the most common being sexual harassment and domestic violence. This neglect should not be surprising. Most studies are based on official statistics, and incidents of harassment and domestic violence are often either not counted as crime or never reported to the police. Yet practically all the teenagers and young adult women and even some of the senior women interviewed during this study reported some experience with sexual harassment. The most common forms were being chased and receiving unwelcome comments, touches, and insults in school, at work, or while walking on the streets. One of the most important findings of this study is that many women report being sexually harassed—and that these acts of aggression are connected to the sentiments of anger, apprehension, worry, concern, and fear that women experience. Several middle-class, suburban African American teenagers clearly expressed their feelings during a group discussion. Talking over each other, they said:

As far as the school goes, what worries me is sexual harassment.

I asked, "From whom, from boys, professors?"

Mainly from boys.

Although there is a teacher. He is the physical education director.

I hate the way the boys talk to girls. They say any kind of things that make you feel uncomfortable. We had a film that made me realize about sexual harassment. I mean . . . I didn't realize how many times somebody . . . a male makes me feel uncomfortable.

I have been harassed like . . . you know. . . . I was at the high school when I felt in my butt or something.

And then they say things like . . . if you wear tight jeans . . .

If you have that, the way they look at you is like if you were a pork chop or something walking in front of them.

I don't even know who he was. We were . . . it was after we had a basketball game or something, and this guy, I don't even know who he was. It was him and two other people, and we walked by. And I had the feeling that they would harass us. And he was like . . . he slapped me on my behind. Now he even jokes about it, all the time . . . I turned around in slow motion and looked at him. And it was like . . . OH MY GOD! . . . I was like in shock. It was like someone had violated me.

When a guy verbally sexually harasses you . . . I don't know. I don't say anything, because I don't want to make him upset like creating a scene and he may physically hurt you.

You know what makes me nervous? Is when a guy tries to talk to you and you don't really want to talk to him but . . . you don't want them angry.

If you say, "No, I don't want to talk to you," they act like if you were so rude and they will start to do things and they may hit you, pull out a gun. You don't know what they might do.

The same teenagers expressed their feelings toward a teacher who "has a reputation among the girls" of molesting them:

When I wore a short skirt, one time, Mr. G. was making comments about it and like he was really . . . and I don't like that. He is supposed to be a man and he plays a pervert, seriously. He is supposed to be a teacher.

Many women report being followed on the streets, stared at, or insulted because they do not respond to an unwelcome advance. Sexual harassment is so prevalent that to some women it seems as if it is nothing out of the ordinary. Lynette, a twenty-three-year-old African American participant, claimed:

The only harassment that I can think of is the normal, the basic . . . hey baby! . . . And I hate it . . . it makes me feel angry. I feel like if I have been punched.

Although Lynette was very clear in her statement that these comments upset her, she considered them "normal," given the fact that they are part of the everyday experience of most women. Some of these incidents, however, can be especially traumatic to some women. A twenty-one-year-old African American woman described a frightening incident on the subway:

This man was very close to me. He whispered in my ear, "I want to rape you and hear you scream." The scariest thing was that I was in a crowded subway in the middle of the day. However, I was so scared to be sexually assaulted. This was very spooky. Usually, someone brushes up against you for a little too long, and you start to get uncomfortable. I believe that women are victimized everyday by these little rapes.

Women reported being harassed regardless of their race, socioeconomic background, or place of residence. Hillary, a thirty-five-year-old white middle-class professional woman who dresses in suits and conservative outfits, recounted an incident that occurred in one of the fanciest areas of Manhattan, Park Avenue:

The men around my home are business men . . . and I am still hearing things. Like if they feel, "I have all the money I want and I can treat you like shit, because I am in control." That is the type of man that I am afraid of. I have seen the construction workers doing it. . . . But, the men that have money . . . they think that they can get away because they have money and power . . . that makes me be afraid of them. . . . I was on Park Avenue and 32nd street with a notebook. I was going to school. And this Cherokee Jeep drove up next to me, and they offered me a ride. "No, thanks," I said, "I am waiting for a taxi." Then, they just asked me, "How much would you charge for giving us a blow job?"

Women are more afraid of crime than men, even though official statistics show that they are less likely to be victims of a crime (Warr 1984). This so-called paradox of fear puzzles many criminologists, but it certainly does not puzzle feminist researchers (Stanko 1991), or women in general, who are familiar with the everday acts of hostility committed against them. Sexual harassment has been defined as the "unwanted imposition of sexual requirements in the context of a relationship of unequal power" (Andersen 1993). Acts of sexual harassment, which some find innocuous, are constant reminders that men have power over women's lives; that if they feel like touching a woman, they can do so without any consequence; and that if they are rejected, as one of the students mentioned, they have the right to be angry and even to become violent. The idea in some of these men's minds seems to be, How dare she reject me? The possibility of aggression that women face when confronted by a harasser is clearly linked to the fears they experience and the control that these fears impose on their lives.

As Marianne Hester (1992, 27–39) observes, "personal relations," at home or on the streets, are "extremely crucial areas for acting out and maintaining male dominance." They help to produce and reproduce an unequal gender system with men at the top and women at the bottom. As one of the African American teenagers mentioned, men have the power to make a woman feel like a "pork chop." This process of treating a woman's body as an object has three basic consequences. One is to dehumanize women, which is always a first step toward domination and violence. Of course, women are not the only ones that have been dehumanized in this culture. Blacks, for example, have been presented at different times in history as "animals," "savages," "out of control," and the like (West 1993). Second, it presents an image of women as seductive beings, necessitating male control (Hester 1992). The message behind these acts of aggression is, "If you wear tight jeans (or a short skirt), then I have the right to slap your bottom and to put you in your place." Finally, sexual harassment implies that women are responsible for their own victimization: "If she didn't wear those tight jeans, nobody would bother her," a Latino male student said in reference to his sister during one of my classes on violence against women at Hunter College.

Intimate Violence and Fear of Crime

Traditional studies on fear of crime have ignored the links between domestic violence and feelings of fear or apprehension on the streets or at work. When I asked about the crimes that interview participant feared the most, a few women mentioned domestic violence. A thirty-five-year-old woman, Ines, asserted in a passionate tone of voice: "What I worry about is walking inside the danger that is in your own home." Four other women mentioned being afraid for friends, sisters, and cousins who were involved in situations of domestic violence. "I worry very much about my sister," one of them said. Women victims of domestic violence indicated that those who experience victimization and threats of victimization from husbands, boyfriends, or lovers feel anxious, fearful, and some of them even "terrified." These women have to face not only the violence at home but also the same violence on the streets that other women face. Lucia, a twenty-five-year-old Latina woman, mother of a five-year-old, related her experience of domestic violence and the fear in which she lives.

After what happen to me, being that somebody that you trust can hurt you, it makes you think, "Would this person come back and do something and retaliate against your family in order to get you?" I mean, if someone you loved before can do that to you, a stranger would not be that hesitant.

Lucia took her husband to court. The evidence against him was overwhelming—pictures, witnesses, marks. Moreover, she was one of the few lucky ones who had the family network to support her emotionally and financially during the trial. Even though her attacker was sent to jail, where he remains, Lucia still closes her windows every day, even during the summer, "even when it is very hot," and checks her house every time she comes in. Her fear, however, is not limited to the possibility of being attacked by her husband at home; she also fears strangers. "If I could not stop my ex-husband," she argued, "how can I stop a stranger?" Given her fears, Lucia confessed that she had the fantasy of "relocating to a small town in the middle of nowhere." She knows, nevertheless, that wherever she goes, her fear will accompany her: "What it comes down to is that the fear does not go away, no matter where you live. It is always going to be with you. . . ." "What is your major fear?" I asked. "I am afraid of being involved in another relationship. I don't want to date anyone."

The words Lucia used to describe her sentiments were "hopeless," "afraid of dying," "weak." An important component of her sentiments is her belief that she failed as a mother because she was battered in front of her five-year-old child, Luis, and she "couldn't do anything to stop it." Consequently, her son is afraid of being alone with her, and ironically he feels more comfortable when he is with a man, "especially with my brother," Lucia told me. By witnessing his mother being badly beaten in front of him, Luis internalized the same message that was given to his mother and that is given to many battered women: I can do anything I want, because I own you. Seeing his mother in a situation of weakness taught Luis that men are in control, that they can overpower a woman. Therefore, men can hurt, but they can also protect him. This sort of experience and the fear it engenders reproduces within the family the same gender hierarchy that exists in the larger society.

Lucia's situation is not unique. In fact, she is probably better off than many of the victims of domestic violence who participated in the study, since her husband will remain incarcerated, at least for a time. She has asked the court to notify her before he gets out of prison. Other women victims of domestic violence expressed similar feelings of fear and despair. Florence, a twenty-four-year-old African American who lives with her boyfriend, also reported living "in panic" and being "afraid of leaving him" because he abuses her physically and sexually. "Every time I come home late," she said, "he inserts his fingers in my vagina to see if I have slept with another man. I fear for my life," she said. There is no doubt that such a situation makes women feel powerless, belittled, insulted, threatened. Studies on fear of crime have consistently ignored the fear of being a victim of domestic violence, the anxiety that living in that situation produces, and the impact of these fears on women's overall fear of crime.

Anther woman, Annette, said that being a victim of domestic violence has affected many areas of her life:

I am always afraid, especially at work because I have read about some women who have been shot at work by their husbands. And even if he only shows up. But what if he makes a big scene . . . you know? I cannot even think about a situation like this. I would be not only afraid and embarrassed. What do you think people at work would say? For sure, they'll say, "Probably she did something wrong." I cannot even sleep sometimes, thinking that he may show up at work.

Not even at work does Annette feel safe. She is worried not only about her husband showing up and making a "big scene" but also about what her coworkers might say. Interestingly, the first thought that crosses her mind in this hypothetical, although not necessarily unlikely situation, is that her coworkers are going to blame her for the marital problems and not her husband, who happens to be the aggressor.

Who Are You Afraid Of?

In almost all instances participants said that they were afraid of acts of aggression committed against them by men. Studies show that men are much more likely to be the offenders in all major crimes. Statistics for 1992 show that of all violent crimes committed by a lone offender, the victim reported the attacker to be a male in 86 percent of the cases (Bureau of Justice Statistics 1994b, 289). One major difference found among the participants in the study, however, was that teenagers occasionally reported being afraid of other female teenagers, while adult and senior women were primarily afraid of males.

Racial and class differences seem to play a fundamental role in acts of aggression committed among female teenagers. Connie, a fourteen-year-old white teenager, related the acts of aggression committed by Latina teenagers against her in the school using a tone that made clear how upset she was. "Do you really want me to tell you?" she asked. "Yes," I said.

I have been called a white bitch, white trash, a whore, a bitch . . . these are basically it. And I have not been called by white girls, I have been called by mostly Hispanic girls toward me. I have been pushed downstairs like if . . . I have been laughed at because I might not dress in that homeboy look.

A group of Latina teenagers in a mainly Black and Latino neighborhood said that they were harassed by teenage African American women. One of them, Elba, said, "You know . . . Black girls don't like us." "Why?" I asked.

Well, they think that Black guys like Latinas. So, they get very nasty. Black guys are always trying to talk to us or telling us things like: *Mira, mira, mami* (look, look, baby). It makes me so mad. . . . They think that we cannot speak English. They think that we are stupid or something.

Another added,

Black girls stick bubble gum in our hair. They get jealous, or something, because of our hair . . . we have long curly hair and we don't have to do nothing to have this hair.

"Are there fights?" I asked. Laughing, she responded, "Many" [showing me her fist]. We fight them . . . when they mess with us."

Several teenagers reported getting involved in physical fights with other girls. A few also claimed to fight against boys, if "they get too nasty." This reflects the fact that in some circumstances young women, especially working-class teenagers, do break some of the norms imposed upon them by a gendered society that permits men, but not women, to get involved in physical quarrels. These teenagers feel that to protect themselves and "to be respected," they need to fight. Otherwise "they jump you and beat you." "You have no choice," one of them concluded.

Limited Lives

The fear of crime limits the lives of the women interviewed in this study in many ways, from the seemingly innocuous rituals of not walking out by themselves at night, to the most constraining: not taking a certain job, not attending night classes, or avoiding the streets completely. Some of these constraints seem also to be related to age and socioeconomic status. Teenagers and young adults were more likely to use expressions such as, "You cannot let fear stop you." Some of the older women's lives, on the other side, were highly constrained by their anxieties. Barbara, an elderly Latina woman, said, "I do not go out of my apartment; if I have to buy something, I ask my son to do it." Several senior and adult women mentioned that they do not go out at night.

The right to the use of public space is limited for women. Most participants avoid places such as parks and certain neighborhoods. As Gloria said, "I used to go and walk around the Village at night, forget it. . . . No, I wouldn't do it." Two women said that they were afraid to drive by themselves. According to Cecilia,

Even when I drive, my biggest fear is running out of gas or having an emergency come up or falling asleep at the wheel of the car. I am afraid of driving alone.

At least five women said that they do not take the train and prefer the bus. Those who can afford to take a taxi at night do it. This means that fear of crime also has economic consequences for women, who have to pay more money for transportation in order to feel safe.

Several students said that they do not take night classes and base their choice of schools on the availability of safe transportation. Even when she wanted to attend another school, Sue, a twenty-two-year-old white student, concluded:

That school was out of the question because it was too far from my home and I would feel very unsafe having to go there every day.

One twenty-nine-year-old Black woman of Caribbean descent, Louise, explained how she changed her class schedule because of the fear that some incidents provoked in her:

I was followed from the #6 to the E and J trains, which is my usual route every single day because of sexual advances and other incidents that happen to me. I have decided since then not to take any classes after 6:00 p.m. because I had a horrible experience that haunts me until this day. . . . A man exposed himself to me and began to tell me horrible things. . . . It did happen a second time, again, the same person around the same time. . . . The most shocking thing to me is that it was a person of the same ethnic group as me. I still cannot understand because that is not part of my culture. I truly believe that it is something that he learned here in America. Everything changed since then because I expected that if something happen to me, my own ethnic group would protect me instead of scaring me to death. I have never reported this to the police, but I think I should.

Two women reported having changed their jobs for fear of commuting by themselves. One of them said, "Your life is more important than a job." Two others said that they did not take certain jobs because they involved night shifts. Finally, one thirty-three-year-old woman, Emma, said that she did not take a job that she liked because it was located in a "bad neighborhood."

A group of Latina teenagers mentioned that they love to dance but don't go to clubs anymore because of what could happen there. Two of them said that even if they wanted to go, "My parents don't let me go." In general, Latina teenagers were more likely to report that their parents limited their behaviors for fear that something could happen to them, although a few of the white teenagers reported similar constraints. Finally, a twenty-five-year-old white woman, Rachel, said that she does not like to go shopping unless accompanied by her husband. She also mentioned being apprehensive when she goes with her small daughter because of "all the stories of kids being abducted at the malls." Rachel is not alone in her fears. According to a recent poll by America's Research Group (Charleston, South Carolina), a survey of 1,003 consumers found that 21.1 percent made fewer trips to stores in the past year because of the fear of crime (*Advertising Age* 1994).

Finally, for some women fear is so pervasive that it seriously interferes with the quality of their lives. Cora, a seventy-four-year-old Puerto Rican woman, said that because she was old and "not as strong or as quick as I used to be," her life has been seriously limited:

This fear has stopped me from enjoying my retirement in that I have to be careful of what I do.

A group of elderly white women said that the fear of crime limits their participation in church and community activities. "I am afraid of going to church meetings during the night," said Rosa. One of the elderly Latina women also mentioned that she does not recycle her cans, bottles, and newspapers because of her fear of going to the basement of her public housing apartment. "The dumpsters are in the basement and I don't go there by myself. I am not crazy," she concluded. The fears that these women shared with me reflect that half of the U.S. population, who are supposedly guaranteed freedom, live imprisoned in the invisible cages of their worries, anxieties, concerns, and fears. Women's lives are highly constrained by the violence and harassment that they have to face daily in their homes, workplaces, schools, and on the streets. They are also affected by the images and representations depicted by an ideology of crime that supports and feeds such violence. Some women's fears have been influenced by previous victimization: mugging, rape, burglary, assault, purse snatching. Most feel vulnerable because being women almost guarantees that they will be harassed, stared at, followed, or molested in the streets. A few say that being victims of domestic violence has made them more afraid. Other women feel particularly vulnerable because of who they are: immigrant women who do not speak English, older women who depend on their welfare checks, African American women whose sons have been harassed by the police.

None of the women interviewed in this study identified herself as a lesbian, nor did I ask about the sexual orientation of participants. Incidents of violence and fear of those incidents against gays and lesbians, however, have been reported in the literature since the 1970s (Bell and Weinberg 1978; Bohn 1983–84; Chamberlain 1985; Miller and Humphreys 1980). More recently, Gary David Comstock, in his book *Violence Against Lesbians and Gay Men* (1991, 37) details incidents of violence committed against individuals with homosexual orientations. He concludes that more than half of socially active gay men and lesbians who have been surveyed by institutions and organizations have experienced some form of violence. Comstock (1991, 38) also reports that although gay men are more likely to be the victim of violent incidents than lesbians, a larger proportion of lesbians of color experience violence than do white lesbians. Thus, a topic of paramount importance is the study of fear of crime on the lives of gay men and lesbians, taking into consideration class and racial differences.

Chapter Four

Innocent and Culpable Victims

Of course, women have to be more careful than men. We are more likely to be victims of a crime because we are weaker. Everybody knows it. Seriously, what can you do if a man grabs you? Think about it. They are bigger and stronger. Of course, you can try to scream or to run, but your chances are too low. Also, you can get hurt. So, you better think before you do something foolish.

> Gabriela, a twenty-five-year-old
> middle-class Latina who lives in
> northern New Jersey

In a famous 1948 study, *The Criminal and His Victims,* Hans Von Hentig developed a typology of thirteen classes of people who were, for either psychological or social reasons, likely to become the victims of crime. Beniamin Mendelsohn, another early victimologist, introduced an alternative typology that classified victims according to their responsibility for the commission of the crime. These works were followed by various writings that further developed the concept of victim-precipitated incidents (Wolfgang 1958; Amin 1971; Hindelang et al. 1978.) Among the most controversial of the studies was one conducted by Menachem Amin (1971), who, using official statistics, applied a very broad notion of victim-precipitation to cases of rape.

Two major contributions of these early victimological studies were, first, their focus on the victims and on the creation of programs and research aimed at understanding and compensating victims of crimes and, second, the creation in 1966 of the first National Crime Victimization Survey (NCVS). In spite of its contributions, "malestream" victimology did not always work to the advantage of the "forgotten victim." Rather, it helped develop a tendency to "blame the victim" which persists in the discipline even today. Thus, from the beginning, the notion of the culpable victim has been an

71

important component of victimology as a discipline and of our ideology of crime.

Images of culpable victims are by no means limited to academic studies. On the contrary, they are constantly echoed in popular discourse. Cynthia, a middle-class African American woman in her mid-twenties, said to me during an interview:

I tell you the truth: some women ask for it. The things that some women do are weird, or stupid, or something. . . . If you don't take care of yourself, who is going to do it? You know, you hear some women saying that they were raped. But then, if you hear what really happened, you wonder. . . . Like that woman who went to Mike Tyson's apartment. Remember? I don't remember her name. I think that she was a Miss or something . . . Desiree something. . . . Don't you think that she looked for it? I really think so. I tell you, sometimes you feel like . . . [hesitantly] if some women enjoy playing the victim.

Although many women are raped every day in America, the first image that comes to Cynthia's mind is the image of what she considers a questionable rape. According to her narrative, the woman precipitated the act, *à la* Menachem Amin (1971). What is important here is not only Cynthia's willingness to blame the victim, but also her willingness to generalize her opinions about this incident, charging that "some women" enjoy "playing the victim."

During the 1970s the women's movement broke a prolonged silence by bringing into the national agenda issues related to the victimization of women in the private sphere, such as child abuse, incest, rape, and domestic violence. For the first time, women survivors of rape openly discussed their victimization and its effects on their lives. Incest and domestic violence victims joined rape survivors in documenting their experiences in detail and in explaining the physical and emotional consequences of these crimes. This, in turn, led to the development of strong, politically activist views that influenced law making, police training, courtroom dynamics, hospital emergency room services, and many programs directly or indirectly involved in the issue of violence against women. At the same time, feminist criminologists introduced issues of female victimization into criminological discourse. Several members of the first antirape group in the world, Bay Area Women Against Rape, were criminology students putting feminist ideas into practice (Schwendinger and Schwendinger 1991).

Feminist studies also led to the recognition that official statistics, including the National Crime Victimization Survey (NCVS), provide a very limited and biased picture of crime and its victims. By focusing only on the study of "street crimes," official statistics ignore most of the crimes committed against women in the intimacy of their homes. In addition, many crimes committed against women go unreported either to the police or to NCVS.

Some feminist studies placed crimes against women in the context of social control of women. Susan Brownmiller (1975), for example, viewed rape and the threat of rape as a way to keep women in their place. Susan Griffin (1971) linked violence against women to a culture of male domination, in which rape acts as a form of "mass terrorism." Without doubt these studies opened society's eyes to hidden issues of violence against women and demystified the perception of American homes as "safe havens." However, they also contributed to the social construction of women as victims. As Karlene Faith says, "The focus in the literature on the effects of adult male violence on women and children had the sum effect of reifying the female as lacking human agency. Women were no longer so thoroughly objectified as male property, but they were reobjectified as Victim" (Faith 1993, 107). Additionally, most studies focused on sexual crimes committed against women, reinforcing the male-centered idea that what is important about women is their sex (Cain 1989, 3).

These early feminist studies also viewed women victims as a homogenous group, irrespective of class and racial differences. In many instances the experiences of African American and Latina women who have been victims of the most heinous crimes for generations were ignored. With some important exceptions, these studies also tended to disregard the resistance strategies used by many women who struggle against their powerlessness. Latinas, for example, are still conventionally presented as passive, victimized by their partners and by male institutions, especially by the state and the legal system. However, examples of the courage and resistance of Latina women to male oppression in its many forms abound, even when the oppressor is a repressive, brutal, masculinized military state. In Argentina the *Madres de la Plaza de Mayo*, a group of courageous women who still meet weekly in a plaza in Buenos Aires to protest against the "disappearances" of their loved ones at the hands of the military government, are an excellent example of the courage of Latina women even under the most brutal circumstances. The resistance of Guatemalan women, exemplified in the figure of Nobel Peace Prize–winner Rigoberta Menchu, in facing the brutality and genocide against their people is another example of courage in the midst of the most fearful and inhumane situations.

African American women, who for centuries were brutalized, assaulted, and raped, have emerged as a strong voice in the academic and literary world, using their victimizations as a platform from which to raise their voices. In *The Color Purple*, Alice Walker creates the character of Celie, an African American teenager who in spite of the sexual abuse committed against her by her stepfather finds her voice and her strength. Rather than be paralyzed by her fears, Celie writes letters to God and finds in the supportive relationships with other Black women the strength she needs to survive (Walker 1982). Thus women not only resist and refuse to be passive in the face of adversity, but many also fight back. In *Beloved*, Toni Morrison's character, Sethe, an escaped slave, kills her newborn baby as a symbol of the deepest of rebellions: to choose the liberty of death instead of the death of slavery and oppression (Morrison 1994).

In general, a woman who kills her abusive husband is not the passive victim of the aggression perpetrated against her. She is rather the angry person who becomes aware that the abuse is not her fault, that she does not deserve it, and that she lives under a system of social relations whose institutions do not support her. To represent victims of rape and domestic violence as "survivors" adds to the idea of women as passive victims. For to survive means, literally, "to remain alive or existent" (*Webster's New American Dictionary* 1995). Many women are not merely the survivors of rape and violence—they do more than just "remain alive." Some of them become advocates, actively involved—alone or in groups—in resistance to oppression (Faith 1993). Other women, aware of their powerlessness within the social structure, have learned to protect themselves so they do not become victims.

Images of women as victims, however, have a great impact on women's and men's lives, contributing to women's fear of victimization and to the constraints imposed upon their lives. Through these

but "survivor" is preferable to "victim"

images we learn, for example, that women are easy targets of violence, vulnerable, and in need of male protection and that women should limit their behaviors and activities so "nothing bad happens to them." We also learn that the streets are dangerous and that home is safe, although the reality is far different. Not surprisingly, research on fear of crime during the past twenty-five years, which focuses on crime in the street, consistently shows that women fear crime more than men do (Ortega and Myles 1987; Skogan 1986; Warr 1984.)

The Social Construction of the Victim

Almost thirty years ago, Peter L. Berger and Thomas Luckman (1967, 1) noted that the common person "inhabits a world that is 'real' to him, albeit in different degrees. And he 'knows,' with different degrees of confidence, that this world possesses such and such characteristics." The words of Berger and Luckman can be easily applied to some of our most common conceptions about crime and the many intertwining themes and images that shape them. The common person possesses a great amount of "knowledge" about crime. This knowledge is molded by, among other influences, stories, images, and cultural representations of Criminals and Victims. I indicated in chapter 2, how "displaced" public fears about crime and other connected themes shape popular representations of the Criminal. For example, criminals are often represented in popular culture by racially charged images of dark-skinned, economically deprived men who are probably on drugs.

Similar anxieties have also helped to construct the image of the Victim. If being a criminal is anti-American, the typical victim in our fantasies is the representation of the good American, victimized by the forces of evil. Rather than see themselves as victims of economic forces controlled by large economic institutions and political decisions, many Americans blame certain groups for their problems. We have seen how feelings of victimization take different forms. Americans see themselves as victims of poor people and immigrants—and more recently of single teenage mothers—because their taxes are used to pay for social services required by these groups. Nowadays many white men express the view that they are victims of affirmative action policies that have gone "too far" (Berke 1994b, A-21) because "unqualified women and minorities" are given unfair advantages in jobs that rightfully belong to white men—who evidently consider themselves the only qualified candidates (Estrich 1994, 54, 55). Many Americans also feel victimized by the many social maladies blamed on the poor and minorities, especially drugs and crime. Women's liberation takes its share of the blame as well (Faludi 1991). After all, if women were at home, things would be different. And even those women who have to work because one salary is no longer enough to support a family should be at home when the children return from school and should be held responsible for most of the unpaid domestic work. Thus, in more than one way, women *are* at home even though they hold jobs.

Media representations of the Victim are consistent with images of what "being an American" means. The press loves victims if they are white, middle-, or—better—upper-middle-class (Cose 1990, 19). Moreover, the media generally present victims as decent, responsible, hard-working, family-oriented people. On the rare occasions when Latinos and Blacks are represented as victims, they are portrayed as sharing some of these "American" values, unlike the other members of their race: they are harder working, more attractive, better students, or better persons (Cose 1990,19). The killing of Cindy Del Carmen Villalba reflects this trend. On July 15, 1995, the headline of *The Record*, a northern New Jersey newspaper, read: "Mugger Kills Honor Student, 20." According to the newspaper, the victim, a Latina from Paterson, New Jersey, was class valedictorian in high school and "the first member of her family to attend college" (Kunkle 1995, A-1, A-7). The underlying message is that, in spite of being Latina, the victim was an honor student, which makes her different from other members of minority groups, who are typically presented as lazy and uneducated. Therefore, the victim is worthy of the news coverage because she is a "good person" and hence a blameless female victim who was killed by a stranger. But what would happen if she were not an honor student? Would the crime be worth the coverage? What makes a person a worthy or a deserving victim?

Because the mass media idolize upper- and middle-class white victims, public images of the Victim mirror class, race, and, I argue, gender hierarchies. A look at many of the high-profile crimes reported by the media—the killing of Jennifer Levin by Robert Chambers, the case of the Central Park jogger, the murder of Nicole Brown and Ronald Goldman, to name just a few—leaves the false impression that most victims of crime are white, middle-class women. Although the National Crime Victimization Survey indicates that the rate of victimization for Black females (51.5 per 1,000) is higher than for white females (42.9 per 1,000) (Bureau of Justice Statistics 1995a, 233), the media present women of color as victims much less frequently. Perhaps it is because, to sanction rape and sexual exploitation during slavery and thereafter, African American women have been historically portrayed as libidinous, aggressive beings (Mullings 1994, 269). Such images make them *ipso facto* culpable victims. More recently, the related image of Black teenagers as single mothers, promiscuous and probably addicted to crack, further reinforces the image of Black women as culpable victims.

Images of Women as Victims

One of the questions asked of the participants during the research project was, "In your opinion, who is more likely to be the victim of a crime?" Contrary to what the statistics on victimization show, and independent of their age, race, and class, the majority of the respondents said that women were more likely than men to be victims of crime. "Women, of course," Nancy, one of the white participants, unequivocally stated. Only a very small fraction of the women interviewed said that the gender of the person did not matter, and very few said that men were more likely than women to be victims of crime. During a focus group interview with a group of white, middle-class college students, Heather said, "Anyone can be a victim," but "women are definitely more vulnerable to crime than anybody." "The typical victim is for sure a woman," Judith replied. "Can you give me an example?" I asked. Heather responded:

What I have in mind is the group of women who were killed at the University of Florida a couple of years ago. Because my first group of friends had gone to college and I have quite a few friends at the University of Florida and . . . when I think of a victim I think about these women. Because there were four women in their college apartment, getting ready to start a new semester, and *a man living in the woods* came into their home and brutally murdered them. And I think of them as the victims because they are *the average American* living in their house, unaware, unsuspecting about what can possibly happen to them, and just happened [emphasis added].

Heather's story is quite revealing for several reasons. First, from all possible images of victims, she chose to talk about a situation very similar to her own; she was about to start college, as were the women at the University of Florida. This was a typical response. Many of the stories about victims shared by the participants were closely related to the circumstances of the narrator. Second, the criminal Heather described perfectly fits the idea of the Criminal: a stranger—literally—living in the woods, probably unemployed, and "weird." Third, the women in Heather's narrative fit the image of the innocent, or the *average* (a code word for white), American woman involved in a respectable activity. The attack occurred in a place where the victims were supposed to be, and they were not involved in an activity considered inappropriate for women.

Interviewees also frequently mentioned children as victims. One of the most common stories shared by the participants was that of "little children kidnapped by someone driving by." "Children are weaker," said Gabriela, a twenty-seven-year-old Latina. "They are *buenos* (good), *inocentes* (innocent) and do not know about *maldad* (badness)." Thus innocence was an important trait of a victim. Margaret, a white teenager, shared with me her image of the victim:

To me victims are like little Pollyannas. I imagine a blond girl, like . . . from the Midwest, with a ponytail, naive, unaware, walking down the street in New York City, singing laralaralara.

The representations contained in the preceding narrative are particularly relevant for the argument of this book. In them, Margaret summarizes several elements. Besides the innocence and lack of malice expressed in the image of Pollyanna, Margaret chose the figure of a midwestern girl, with a ponytail, the image of what it means to be a "mainstream American girl": a white, blond, good, virginal, family-oriented young woman. The Midwest was called the "heartland of America" by several newspapers in their coverage of the Oklahoma bombing. "What is more American than the Midwest?" the press reported. Moreover, the criminal act that Margaret visualizes occurs in a large urban center, New York City, the ultimate representation of a place where heinous criminal acts are likely to occur.

The polarization of criminal and victim is unmistakable. It is emotionally appealing to represent crime as an epic battle between the forces of darkness and light, with victims as the lambs and criminals the wolves, with victims as innocent and criminals guilty, with victims as women and children and criminals as dark-skinned men. The truth, however, is that such images oversimplify and distort the reality of crime. These representations not only make women more fearful than men; they also lead us to believe that women have a monopoly on submission and men on aggression, that men have control of the streets while women should be sent back home—where they are, in fact, more likely to be victimized.

Although it is true that American society is split along gender lines, women are not the lambs of sacrifice, nor are men the wolves of *Little Red Riding Hood*. The social reality is more complicated than these dichotomies will accommodate. Certainly the relations between men and women occur within the context of gender, class, and race structures, but as Hegelian dialectic teaches us, they cannot be reduced to simplistic notions of "women = victims," "men = victimizers" or "women = good," "men = bad." On the contrary, there are many contradictions involved in male-female relations, with women and men trying to negotiate their places in relationships. In addition, individual male-female relations are influenced by various factors, a major one being control of economic resources. Moreover, these relations are not static; they are in permanent flux. This is why every single exchange between men and women is important, why every single ritual counts: because each contributes to the social evolution of personal and social gender relations. The notion of women as permanently submissive and men as permanently aggressive helps to preserve the gender-based hierarchical system and to promote a conservative mentality in which women are seen as in permanent need of protection and men as permanent protectors.

White Women as Victims

Although a handful of women reported that the race of the victim did not matter, the majority of women reported that white women were more likely to be the victims of crime than Black or Latina women.

Consistent with my hypothesis, white middle-class women fit the image of the innocent victim that prevails in mainstream society's ideology of crime. "White women are more often victims because they do not know how to scream," said Melinda, an African American teenager. Yvette, another of the African American teenagers, expressed her view on who is more afraid of crime: "The majority of the scared women are white, that is the truth. I know that that's true." She claims that white women look scared when passing by Black males and sometimes when passing by Black females, "like us," she concluded. Yvette and the other participants of the focus group are homeless teenagers. Thus, the implication behind Yvette's words is that white women also feel scared of poor Black female teenagers. Some of the Latina teenagers expressed similar ideas. A focus group of Latina teenagers in Brooklyn made these observations:

White women are more victims because they do not know how to fight.

We do; we know how to take care of ourselves.

This is why they do not mess with us.

But white girls are afraid of everybody, of Latinos, of Blacks. This is why they are more victims. They have it worse.

Since I was a little girl, I have had to look after myself. So, I know how to do it. White girls have always somebody looking after them; that is why they don't learn to protect themselves.

The white women described here fit the socially acceptable image of femininity. Since nice girls do not fight, white women are taught not to get involved in physical squabbles. Only bad girls—or girls of color—do. And since middle- and upper-class white America condemns the idea of women becoming involved in physical, and sometimes even verbal, fights, poor women and women of color feel that they have an advantage: they have had to learn how to protect themselves. This makes them the modern witches, afraid of nothing and demonized by the media and by large sectors of the U.S. population.

The virtual absence of Black and Latina women as victims in the media (Benedict 1992, 8, 9) influences fear of crime in several ways. First, the white women in this study more frequently expressed fear of crime than did Black and Latina women. This difference was especially important among teenagers, with white middle-class teenagers expressing more fear than Black and Latina teenagers. Second, the image of white women as innocent victims contains the implicit notion of "white womanhood" as something important to be preserved. The virtue of Black and Latina women is not as important: they are culpable victims because of their race, unless they have some qualities in common with white middle-class victims. To be recognized as victims, Black and Latina women have to show that they are better than the rest of their kind: better mothers, better students, more religious, or more virtuous.

One group of participants who did not uphold the image of white woman as victim were some working-class, Spanish-speaking Latinas who expressed the belief that they were more likely to be the victims of crime. Gisela commented to the group:

We are more likely to be victims. We are *aisladas* [isolated]. We do not live in our countries, and we do not speak English well. That makes us *débiles* [weaker].

Elizabeth, also Latina, shared a story that reflects the isolation and vulnerability that she feels and its relation to her image of the Victim:

I heard an incident in the radio Latina about a woman who was killed in her apartment. She screamed for help and the neighbors heard someone screaming. But, they could not understand what she was saying because she was yelling in Spanish. She was twenty-five years old and she yelled and yelled for help and no one came. They should have come anyway, to see what was happening. But they did nothing.

The relationship between victimization, fear of crime, and immigrant status has not been studied. The words of Elizabeth, however, give us a glimpse of the fears that immigrant women face. Separated from their extended families and their communities, Latinas feel especially *débiles* or vulnerable. Even if they yell for help, their cries are unheard: people cannot understand them. This is an extremely powerful and emotionally appealing representation in the minds of many Latina women. Several of them mentioned the language barrier in association with their fear of crime. Maria and Elena, two Latina women in their thirties, said:

*Me da mucho miedo que alguien me trate de robar y que yo no entienda lo
que ellos quieren* [I am afraid of someone trying to rob me and that I cannot
understand what they want from me]. *Esta idea me aterroriza porque me
pueden hasta matar* [this idea terrifies me because they can even kill me].

Sí, nosotras estamos muy limitadas, porque no sabemos la lengua [Yes, we
are very limited because we don't speak the language]. *Si algo nos pasa no
podemos ni pedir ayuda* [if something happens to us we cannot even ask for
help]. *El otro día me robaron la cartera y, pues, que iba yo a hacer? Como
no tengo ni papeles, me quedé con la rabia* [The other day they stole my purse
and, What am I supposed to do? Since I don't have documents, I just kept
my anger to myself]. *Ahora tengo más miedo, pero me cuido más* [now I am
more afraid, but also more careful].

Undocumented women are especially vulnerable because they cannot report their victimization to the police for fear of deportation. They
must therefore remain silent about the crimes committed against them
at home and in the streets. As Elena suggests, this makes them more
fearful and more cautious, limiting their lives even more severely.

A Dichotomy of Victimhood

Images of the Victim are not unidimensional. They can be placed
along a continuum, with one end representing the good, innocent victim who deserves our tears and the other representing the bad, culpable victim who does not deserve our tears. Such labels are assigned to
victims not only by the media, but also by the public. Eventually, they
become part of the way victims are represented in popular discourse,
helping to mold the ideological constructs of crime. Some victims may
be placed between the two extremes. The Central Park jogger, for example, was labeled "stupid" for jogging in Central Park after dark.
She shared many of the qualities of the innocent victim; she was a
white, upper-middle-class stockbroker, hard-working and responsible, but she could not be entirely innocent because she was somewhere she shouldn't have been. An innocent victim needs to watch
where she goes, with whom she associates. She must not violate clear
norms regarding "proper" places and "proper" people.

By *innocent victims* I do not mean people who are *real* victims of a
certain type of crime or are at risk of becoming victims of crime. I

refer instead to our perception, molded by the ideology of crime, that certain people are likely to become victims. My definition of the innocent victim is analogous to Nils Christie's concept of the "ideal victim," or "a person or a category of individuals who—when hit by crime—most readily are given the complete and legitimate status of being a victim" (1986, 18–30). The typical image of the ideal victim is the innocent person who is robbed, assaulted, mugged, or killed, but who cannot be blamed for his or her own victimization. Several narratives in our culture reveal popular images of the ideal victim. One example is the elderly woman who, while taking care of her sick sister, goes to the bank in the middle of the day to get money to buy medicine and is assaulted by an "ideal criminal," stereotypically represented by the image of a Black man who grabs her purse and drags her into the middle of the street where she is hit by a passing car. The man is a known junkie who uses the money to buy drugs.

In many instances, these labels are formalized in the courtroom, where defense attorneys attempt to demonstrate the innocence of an alleged perpetrator by showing how culpable the victim is. In the famous O.J. Simpson case, for example, Nicole Brown was portrayed as the culpable victim because she was not monogamous—she had several lovers, she was a party girl, she drank and did drugs. As a result, she could not be a good mother, and "she drove O.J. crazy," as a young man recently told me.

There are many examples of the innocent victim. Children and older women victims of heinous crimes shape the bulk of these representations. One of the women interviewed, Marcia, shared with me in her narration her image of the innocent victim. With a tone of voice that showed her profound distress, she said:

Remember that girl? Polly Klaas? She was kidnapped from her home in California by a man who killed her. Her picture was all over the place. I believe that she was in her room, playing with other girls. To me that's the worst that can happen to anyone. Imagine her poor parents.

This heinous crime received a great deal of attention by the media and prompted "three-strikes-and-you're-out" laws around the country ("Jury Selection Begins in the Polly Klaas Case," *New York Times,* 12 July 1995, A-12). In the case of Polly Klaas, the innocent victim is a twelve-year-old middle-class white girl who was in the place where she should have been—her bedroom—and in the company of other innocent girls when she was attacked by a faceless stranger coming out of the shadows.

Polly Klass's murder was, indeed, hideous. Of the thousands of crimes committed in the United States every day, however, only a handful become news. These are chosen because they are believed to excite the public's emotions and, most important, because they sell. They also contribute to the production of a "mass-mediated visual culture" that feeds and is fed by dominant assumptions about crime, criminals, and noncriminals; victims and nonvictims (Barak 1994b, 3). Through these representations of the innocent victims a complex web of images, themes, concepts, and codes are embedded in our subconscious minds, helping to construct a shared version of the social reality that feeds our fantasies and anxieties. These mass-mediated themes teach us what crimes to fear the most, what persons to be afraid of, where or when to be afraid, who is more likely to be a victim, and who is an innocent or a culpable victim.

Another theme that was mentioned by some participants was the relation between body size and victimhood. Although there are no studies on body size and fear of crime, short women do match society's images of weakness and vulnerability. In Jody's words,

I think small women, like me. I think the size has a lot to do with it. Tiny women, like me, are more likely to be victims. Especially tiny women who walk around looking as if they are totally out of it.

As we will discuss later, several women also reported feeling more protected when accompanied by a tall man. Shortness and tallness, I believe, have to do with qualities regarded as feminine and masculine in our culture. Cinderella had small feet, symbolizing her femininity. Songs in Spanish popular culture talk of small women, with *cinturas y pies pequeños* (small waists and feet) as the personification of the "perfect woman."

Contrary to the reality of crime, another pervasive belief among the participants was that victimization was "a random thing; even an eighty-year-old woman can be raped," Norma, an elderly white woman, emphatically asserted. "It can be anybody that happens to be in the path," she concluded. Children were especially represented as victims of random violence, although the reality is that many acts of victimization against children occur at the hands of their parents or guardians. A study by Richard Gelles and Murray Strauss (1979, 15-39), for example, showed that between 1.4 and 1.9 million children in the United States are victims of physical abuse by their parents every year. What is important, however, is not what is "real," as Berger and Luckman have said, but what people *know* as reality—or common-sense knowledge—in their everyday lives (1967, 15).

Sexuality and Sexual Attack

Many of the participants in this study referred to women as victims of murders or sexual attacks, specifically rape, although a few mentioned sexual harassment on the streets as a form of victimization. In fact, women are more likely to be victims of property crimes, muggings, and domestic violence, yet the media continually depict women as predominantly victims of sexual attacks. This image reinforces the idea that what is most important about women is their sexuality (Faith 1993).

Images of "virgin or vamp," as the title of Helen Benedict's book (1992) indicates, reinforce negative stereotypes of women as seductresses, modern Eves who are, in many cases, to be blamed for their own victimization. The January 15, 1996, edition of *Newsweek* gives a vivid example of the dichotomous representations of women in the media. The first lady, Hillary Rodham Clinton—who has become the target of attacks by members of the Republican party—is featured on the cover. Two words are printed below her picture in white and red letters, reflecting the stereotypical images often used by the media to describe women: "Saint or Sinner?"

A large number of women in the study asserted that women who dress provocatively are to be blamed for their own victimization. A group of elderly middle-class white women discussed their views in this way:

This may be old-fashioned thinking too . . . what I have heard through the years. . . . You take the young girls today . . . I think . . . oh! they are inviting trouble. . . . Look how some of them act when they are out on the streets . . . how they dress, leaving nothing to the imagination, and I only think about what my mama used to say . . . you know? They are looking for trouble. A decent girl should not dress like that.

Yes, I agree. Especially in these days women use these tights, showing everything. And then they complain if men look or touch them or if they tell them something they don't want to hear.

Especially some of the young . . . well, Black and Hispanic girls. They like to wear those very tight pants . . . or too-short miniskirts.

They look for it. Yes, I think they like the attention. And men, you know how they are. . . . These women are inviting them.

These expressions imply that women who do not follow a certain dress code are to be blamed for the harassment and attacks that they receive. Also, such statements are consistent with class and racial stereotypes associated with the culpable victim. White middle-class women dress decently; lower-class Black and Latina women, as a participant in the focus group mentioned, like to show their bodies; they are "vamps."

Young, lower-class Latina and African American women, overall, expressed the belief that a woman has the right to dress the way she wants. Clara, an African American teenager, was emphatic in her assertion that "we are not harming anybody, you know." "I dress the way I want," she concluded. Other expressions used by Latina teenagers were, "A woman has the right to dress the way she wants"; "Men dress the way they want, no?"; or "no matter the way you dress, men harass you anyway, so why bother?" Middle-class African American teenagers, however, were more cautious in expressing their belief that "women should dress the way they want." "Men follow girls that dress as a hooker," Melinda claimed. Finally, a frequent response among all women participants was that women who show their jewelry or flash their money, who are not cautious, "look scared, insecure," or are "naive and stupid" are in some ways inviting their own victimization. "Not that they deserve it," said Ivelisse, but "it is very real. You have to watch for yourself."

Many of these images have permeated the criminal justice agencies that deal with crime, criminals, and their victims. Police officers frequently blame women for their own victimization. One of the participants related an incident that happened to her sister, who was raped by a stranger who broke into her apartment while she was sleeping. According to her account, some of the questions asked by the police had an accusatory tone: "What were you wearing while you were sleeping?" "Do you usually sleep in the nude or do you wear pajamas?" "What color underwear were you wearing?" Although the crime happened in the middle of August during a very hot night, she was asked, "Why was your window open?" Some questions may be necessary to determine the circumstances surrounding a crime, but the police should be sensitive enough to ask them in a tone that does not imply accusation, as their questions often do.

Toward a Typology of Female Victims

Images of innocent and culpable female victims are clearly distinguished by a myriad of attributes. Table 2 presents eight characteristics that shape some of the major themes that emerged during this study. These characteristics are embedded in the social construction of the innocent and the culpable victim. Because these are ideal types, some cases may not strictly fit the two outermost points of the continuum of guilt on the one hand and innocence on the other. However, it is my argument that in the case of female victimization, public discourse often becomes very polarized: female victims are virgin or whore, saint or demon, Pollyanna or bitch.

As Table 2 shows, the innocent victim is usually a respectable woman, often married with children or a widow. If she is "still" single, she is either young and a virgin or she has a steady boyfriend. As reported by several of the participants, the attack on the innocent victim usually occurs while she is driving her kids to school, going to work or classes, or, better still, going to church. "That poor lady who was shot in my neighborhood," Ramira, one older Latina told me, "you won't believe it. She was shot on her way to church."

Thus the innocent victim cannot be blamed for being at the place of the attack at that particular time, because she is merely carrying out her responsibilities as a mother, worker, student, housewife, or religious, family-oriented person. She cannot defend herself against the attack because she is weaker than the attacker(s), or if she tries, she is overpowered. "Women are weaker"; "Even if we try, men are

TABLE 2.   Typology of Female Victims

The Innocent Victim	*The Culpable Victim*
She is a respectable woman.	She is a woman of dubious reputation.
She was attacked while she was engaged in a respectable activity.	She was attacked while engaged in an activity considered improper for women.
The place and time of her attack are considered appropriate for a woman.	She was at a place and/or a time considered unsafe for women.
She is weaker than her attacker.	She is strong and she could have protected herself.
She wears conservative or modest clothes and jewelry.	She dresses in a provocative or revealing manner, improper for a decent woman.
She associates with other respectable women and men.	She associates with the wrong crowd.
She was attacked by an "ideal criminal," a stranger.	She was attacked by one of her disreputable friends or by a disreputable stranger.
The attack was vicious, resulting in serious injury or death.	Even if she was hurt, she exaggerated or fabricated the nature of the attack.

much stronger"; and "Once you are in the situation, there is nothing you can do" were among the most common phrases used to express the belief that women cannot defeat men.

As several of the participants expressed, the innocent victim dresses in a very conventional manner: her dress does not show cleavage, and she wears neither "provocatively" tight pants nor too short a skirt. Since she is a "respectable" person, she is involved in activities with other conventional people. The attacker is usually a disreputable stranger who came from nowhere, lurking in the shadows, waiting for his prey. As a result of the attack, the victim was seriously injured, raped, or even killed. As I will discuss in the next chapter, many of the narratives shared by the participants included images of the deranged stranger as criminal.

In contrast, the culpable victim is usually demonized as a woman who is involved in sexual relations with various men. If she has children, she is probably a single mother and neglects them by going out and leaving them alone. She is poor, possibly on welfare. At the moment of the attack, she was in a bar, disco, motel, park, probably drinking or doing drugs, and, very likely, she would have had a sexual encounter. In the words of Myrna, a white woman in her sixties:

> You hear all these stories. Some women go out with a friend and then they drink too much and put themselves in some kind of situations. . . . Then, if the man wants something from them, they get upset. What do they expect? Why put yourself in that situation?

As several participants reported, the culpable victim dresses in a provocative way. She is known to be involved with drug dealers, men and/or women of dubious reputation, probably unemployed. Her place of residence is either unknown or she lives in a "bad neighborhood." She was raped or assaulted by a friend/lover/husband or she looked for it, and now she claims that she was seriously hurt, but she is crying wolf. In the conventional phrase some of the participants used to characterize these images, "She asked for it."

The images of innocent and guilty victims have a great impact on our lives. They are part of the ideological repertoire about crime that teaches us, from a very early age—often subconsciously and cumulatively—that there are two kinds of victims: the deserving and the undeserving. The first has our compassion and our tears; the second, our indifference and sometimes even our animosity. But these images teach us more than compassion for some victims or disdain for others. They also teach us that some crimes committed against women are not "real" crimes, because they are not committed by strangers, as in marital rape; because they occur in a place where the victim should not be, such as Mike Tyson's hotel room; and because the woman did not end up in the hospital, as in many acquaintance rapes. Second, they set limits on our actions by establishing a strict code of behavior that leads us to believe that "respectable women" do not go to certain places, do not dress in certain ways, and do not associate with the "wrong" people. They shape our fear of crime, imposing boundaries on our actions and organizing public consent around issues of "women's proper behavior."

Interestingly, the woman who is not a victim has many of the qualities of the "good victim": she is respectable and engages only in respectable activities, she does not frequent certain places at certain times, she is feminine and weak, she dresses in a conventional manner, and, of course, her friends are all respectable. The only difference is that the nonvictim did not have the bad luck of being randomly attacked by a lunatic. As Pilar, one of the participants in the study said:

You just have to prevent something from happening. I know that I am extremely careful. I don't dress provocative, I don't go out at night by myself, I don't go to dangerous places, I don't wear jewelry. If I go out I do not drink. What for? Better safe than sorry. If something happens it's just bad luck, but I don't take any chances.

Not coincidentally, the good victim and the nonvictim share many of the qualities that the conservative ideology attributes to a traditional, family-oriented, white middle-class woman. These are the images that women should aspire to, so nothing bad will happen to them. The motto is: If you do not want to be a victim, then be a good girl and follow the rules.

Since we are taught that criminals are the vicious strangers that lurk in the woods—the psychopath, the unemployed, the alcoholic or drug addict who comes from the shadows—we must avoid them as much as we can. Therefore, we are told, stay safe, be a good girl, avoid the woods. Depictions of women as victims of strangers are the lifeblood of the social control that fear of crime imposes on our lives. Since representations of the victim mirror multiple and overlapping social hierarchies—hierarchies of race, gender, and class—it is no coincidence that images of the innocent victim are more concordant with the characteristics of the white middle-class female. In this society, white women have more opportunities to obtain an education and therefore to become "respectable" college students or to have "respectable" jobs. White women are also more likely to be considered "feminine," according to dominant media images, and to dress in a middle-class, Protestant, conservative manner. They usually wear discreet jewelry, if any: small pearl earrings, never large gold ones. Naturally, they associate with respectable men and women. Since popular representations of innocent victims mirror images of white middle-class women, frequently older or very young, and since these images surround us from a very early age, it should not be surprising that some studies show that those who share the characteristics of an innocent victim—older middle-class respectable white women—are also more afraid of crime (Christie 1986, 27). At a subconscious level, fear of crime serves to present the virtue and purity of middle-class white women as the ideal to which all of us, white women and women of color, should aspire.

Truly, the media are not the only ones to convey these images, to feed our fantasies and make us more fearful. There are other no less effective and powerful ways in which we are trained to fear. Fairy tales and bedtime stories, for example, very powerfully transmit the ideology of crime and victimhood, teaching us to react to victimization with fear and passivity. These stories are filled with images of women as innocent, fearful victims who react passively to their misfortune, often by literally staying inside, as we are commanded to do today. Sleeping Beauty is the perfect victim who reacts to her tragedy by staying at her castle in near-death paralysis for one hundred years! Her only responsibility is to be beautiful and wait. Snow White also remains passive, inert inside her crystal coffin until the Prince appears. Little Red Riding Hood, one of the few who defies the order to stay in by taking food to her ill grandmother—a very respectable activity—pays for her boldness, or perhaps her stupidity, by being attacked. She is so afraid, however, that she cannot fight back, for the wolf is stronger and bigger than she. Interestingly, even Cinderella, who is abused by her stepmother, stays in! Does she try to leave her abuser? No, she waits patiently until Prince Charming rescues her from the adverse situation. In contrast, the male victims in fairy tales act with courage and determination. They encounter giants and are swallowed by whales, but they face their victimization and adversity bravely. The reaction of the Three Little Pigs is quite different from that of Little Red Riding Hood. Their survival skills are clearly highlighted in the story. They know how to protect themselves against the attacks of the Bad Wolf (Brownmiller, 1975, 310).

Hollywood's films also teach women to fear. Jack the Ripper, the misogynist killer who, in the autumn of 1888, mutilated and murdered his victims, terrifies us. Several films and books produced about him and his crimes unveil the story of the five prostitutes who walked London's streets unaware of the fate that awaited them. The Ripper figure has inspired many other movies and books, becoming a powerful myth and contributing to the construction of modern imagery of male criminals and female victims in movies and novels, feeding our contemporary ideology of crime and victims. The Ripper myth has especially nourished our fears because his identity remains unknown, his face a mystery. He is the perfect faceless stranger who attacks his victims and is never caught. But he is also the lone ranger who launches a war against society's moral decay by killing prostitutes or "bad, culpable and undeserving victims" (Bland 1992). As in traditional victimology, the Ripper also teaches us that some women "ask for it" and that bad girls are eventually caught in a web of their own making.

Another example can be found in Alfred Hitchcock's movie *Psycho*. The famous scene in which a woman is attacked by a maniac while taking a shower scared a whole female generation. The fact that the woman had embezzled money from her company and moved to another town to "liberate" herself and begin a new life with her boyfriend is not coincidental. She was, indeed, punished for her audacity. For several days, if not weeks, after seeing the movie, my little sister had to be inside the bathroom while I was taking a shower, just to make sure that no one would attack me in such a vulnerable situation. Several women of my generation report similar reactions to the movie. We have been taught to look under the bed, in the closet, in the dark, for strangers, maniacs, psychopaths, dark-skinned men.

Ideologies of crime and the fear of crime have helped to foster a conservative moral agenda in which women are told to protect themselves and their children by assuming traditional roles and by adhering to specific standards of behavior that are considered appropriate. "Conservatives always have the advantage . . . because they can play on fear," said *Village Voice* reporter C. Carr (995, 26–30). Although statistics show that women are less likely to be incarcerated than men, the reality is that women do not need to be incarcerated: they already live in prisons whose walls are invisible and impalpable but inescapable. These prisons seem so natural that only on rare occasions do we question them. And those who dare to ignore them are the new "witches," who, like Clara, the clairvoyant in Isabel Allende's book, *The House of the Spirits* (1993), are afraid of nothing.

Some women refuse to give up activities that are important to them or to change their lives for fear of crime. For example, author Andrea Todd (1994, 30), who runs every night in Riverside Park, New York City, writes: "My friends look on in blank-faced dismay as I lace my running shoes; they plead with me not to go. When I reach for my Walkman, it's the last straw; they tell me dryly that I might as well take along some ID too." Ms. Todd continues, "Everyone says I am asking for it." She emphatically concludes by saying, "However, *to start living like a victim to avoid becoming one is not the solution*" (emphasis added). Comments like this, however, were not common among the participants in this study. Unfortunately, many women do live like victims, constrained within the walls of their invisible prisons.

Chapter Five

The Creation of Outlaws

My image of a criminal . . . is a group of teenagers attacking someone randomly. Like . . . once I saw on the subway a group of Black and Latino teenagers getting into the train, drinking beer and running back and forth while others swung from the poles. They had knives hanging from their jeans. One of them opened a six-inch blade and began to swipe the air. Then he used it to clean his fingernails. After a moment . . . he flung it across the car and it slid against the door. I was scared to death. These are criminals, no doubt about it.

> Pier, a twenty-four-year-old white female who lives in Brooklyn, New York

A criminal to me is someone with a raspy voice, hiding in the dark and waiting for someone in an empty street. As you walk, he approaches you from behind . . . with a knife. He wears a cap or one of those sweatshirts with a hood and has a scar on his face and looks really spooky.

> Laurie, a fifteen-year-old Black female who lives in Queens, New York

I am afraid of those men who rape their wife and children. I was married to one of them. He was very violent. *Me pegaba todo el tiempo* [he used to beat me all the time]. *El es para mí un criminal de lo peor* [he is for me the worst type of criminal]. I don't trust men.

> Claudia, a thirty-five-year-old Latina who lives in a small suburban town in northern New Jersey.

Our ideologies of crime are shaped by a set of images—a cluster of themes, symbols, and codes regarding criminals and victims, crime and its causes, punishment and crime control (Hall et al. 1978, 139). In today's predominantly conservative atmosphere, these images have been inextricably linked to larger social issues of civic order, morality, and family values. In the United States, the discussion about crime is currently being held within the parameters set by a conservative view that focuses on the need for individual attributes such as self-restraint, self-reliance and personal responsibility, ignoring society's own incessant contribution to the causes of crime. Such ideologies help to organize and structure public discourse. They constitute an unquestioned creed that has become a source of "collective emotional force and appeal" (Hall et al. 1978, 140). For example, without questioning the validity of her argument, one of the participants told me in an emotion-filled voice:

Everyone knows that the only thing that works is to send criminals to prison for a long time. Don't you think? . . . You are a criminologist. You know about these things more than I. We need to punish them in a way that scares the shit out of them. They need to know that if they commit other crimes, they are going to stay in prison forever. We need to scare them. Period. The problem is that we are too soft with criminals.

Themes about crime are emotionally captivating. They not only organize consent around "everyone-knows" issues, such as punishment, victims, and criminals, but they also touch fundamental values in the American psyche—nationalism, the work ethic, individual independence, discipline. Contrary to what some may contend, understanding crime is not simply a matter of determining what is intrinsically "wrong" or "right." If this were the case, then one might ask: Why are some behaviors considered criminal, or wrong, by some groups and not by others? Whose definition of right or wrong prevails? A few examples will suffice to make this point: Issues such as abortion, homosexuality, and marijuana use are only some of the most current controversial topics that divide American public opinion. Moreover, what is considered wrong (or criminal) also changes according to historical circumstances. During Prohibition, for example, alcohol drinking was defined as criminal behavior.

Some sociologists, such as social structuralist Emile Durkheim (1982), have advanced the idea that crime should be viewed as a functional rather than a moral phenomenon. Crime helps to create limits or boundaries by defining what behaviors a society is unwilling to tolerate. Such definitions of deviance and deviants are historically and culturally determined. During World War II, for example, Japanese

Americans were placed in internment camps in the United States. They were considered enemies because the United States was at war with Japan. Japanese immigrants were therefore seen as outlaws. Today, Japanese people are perceived completely differently as hard-working, self-disciplined, law-abiding individuals.

As many sociologists have suggested, in the process of creating outlaws, we also create social identity (Chancer 1992, 159, 160; Durkheim 1982; Erikson 1966; Sagarin 1975). The creation of the outlaw, or the other, brings together members of society in a common conviction, to direct their disapproval against those who are outside the social boundaries. Fear is a very important component in the creation of outlaws: we should fear them because they are dangerous, or evil, or just threatening to "us." The production of such a fear is vital not only to organize consent about wrong or right issues, but also to encourage the development of repressive measures to purge or eradicate outlaws. The definition of the Jew as outlaw, for example, both contributed to the creation of the consciousness of being a German and justified the extermination of six million Jews during World War II. Thus, the invention of the outlaw, as Lynn Chancer says (1992, 160), "becomes suggestive in certain occasions more than others," with relations of dominance and submission playing a determining role in their definition. The definition of an outlaw varies according to historical momentum and the needs of society.

The Criminal as Outlaw

What current circumstances are helping to produce a definition of the criminal as outlaw? How are images of the criminal as outlaw embedded in the psyche of women? What is the relationship between these images and the fear of crime among women?

The increased economic inequality of the 1990s has had profound implications in the production of the outlaw. Resources and opportunities believed in the past to be the patrimony of all Americans— health care, education, social security, a steady job—are becoming limited to certain persons. The need to define who "belongs" and who does not has become crucial in current circumstances, because it has profound implications: those who belong will more likely benefit from the scarce resources. Only "real Americans" have the right to the scant entitlements. And, in a society deeply divided according to class, race, and gender, those benefits will be distributed accordingly. Therefore, racial, class, and gender lines need to be bolstered.

The discourse about crime and the fear of crime contributes to the production of the outlaw, the one who is outside the boundaries of a civil society. The fear-producing outlaw is exemplified in the image of the stranger, the dark-skinned man who haunts us from the shadows of alleys and public parks. This image is created and recreated in everyday conversations about criminals as men from other races, possibly immigrants, and certainly poor. We stare daily at the outlaw, who glances back, menacing us from our TV screens and from magazines and newspapers, invading our homes and saturating our imaginations. Fear of crime grants members of society the occasion to legitimize social hierarchies by generating a class, racial, and gendered discourse without being openly racist, classist, and sexist. When confronted with the issue of race and crime, for example, Naomi, a white middle-class woman in her fifties, told me: "Black men have to get their act together. They are killing each other every day in the streets of America." Naomi's words reflect a lamentable reality. Black-on-Black crime is indeed a serious problem in this country (Mann 1993, 46). Yet Naomi's statement contained an implicit generalization about Black people, as if the entire Black race were responsible for the crimes committed by some sectors of the African American population. Narratives such as these ignore the fact that the great majority of African Americans are law-abiding persons. Moreover, when confronted with crimes committed by white people—even serial killers and mass murderers, the majority of whom are white—one rarely, if ever, hears expressions such as, "White people better get their act together."

Gender structures are also recreated in daily conversations when people are confronted with the news of a heinous crime or with the fear of crime. For example, an individual who emphatically declares that a woman has the same right as a man to the use of public space, may say about the crime committed against the Central Park jogger, "Well, what does she think? Doesn't she know that a woman should not go to a public park during the evening?" The implication is that

the rape is at least in part her fault because she was in a place prohib-
ited to women. Similarly, an individual who thinks that a woman has
the same right as a man to hold any job, may tell his partner, "Honey,
I don't think that this job is for you. You would have to travel by yourself, and that can be dangerous for a woman. You know that. When
men see a woman traveling by herself they always try to hit on her.
Do you really want that?" Thus race, class, and gender divisions are
fundamental components of the everyday discourse about crime.

Roseanne, a middle-class white woman in her fifties, shared the
following comment with other participants in a focus group:

> Well, we have to be honest about this. The truth is that most of the crime is
> committed by a very small group of people who act like . . . beasts. And all
> this chat about educating or . . . changing them. I honestly don't think that
> people like that change. It is just a waste of our taxes. What can you do if
> they don't want to help themselves? They don't want to work, like the rest of
> us. I don't want my taxes to be spent on them. Let them sit in prison doing
> nothing. They should be locked up with no TV, nothing.

Then, later in the conversation, she added:

> Come on, let's be honest; the reality is that most criminals are minorities.
> Many of them are people who come to this country thinking that they can
> make it easy. And, do you know? They find that they have to work. Like the
> rest of us. Big deal! It makes me furious.

Comments like this reflect the ways class and race are intercon-
nected in popular discourse. Without using an openly racist or derogatory term, this woman depicted a powerful, emotionally appealing
image of the outlaw. He is a beast, irrational and violent; a stranger,
lower-class, unemployed, different from us. He is a person who cannot be changed, an immigrant or perhaps a member of a minority
group, not someone who believes in the work ethic "like us." Such
images exert a powerful influence on our lives, not only because they
shape our fears about crime, but also because they lead to a call for
the sorts of repressive criminal policies that have been implemented
throughout past centuries.

It became evident throughout this study that regardless of their
own race, women hold strongly racialized images of criminals, with
Black and Latino men at the forefront of most women's fears. During

a discussion with a group of young, educated, middle-class white women, Minna said:

Oh, I just feel bad. I feel that anything that comes to my mind when you ask that question is . . . [hesitantly], I think of a thin, tall Black man. I know that it is a stereotype that is in the media, but that is the image that first comes to my mind.

Lillian and Angela, two of the participants in the same group, concurred:

I hate to say it, but that is exactly what I was thinking.

Me too.

The words of Minna, Lillian, and Angela reflect the deep influence that these images have on people's lives. The three college-educated women understand that they share a stereotypical representation of who a criminal is. Yet awareness does not resolve the problem: The stereotype is still the first picture that comes to mind, shaping our fears and limiting our lives. When we walk down a street and a Black man approaches us, these images "kick in." Although we may remind ourselves that this is only "a stereotype that is in the media," that does not stop our fear or our response: we cross the street or hold our bags tightly, reproducing in this small ritual the same race, class, and gender relations that exist in society at large.

On several occasions, during my class discussions at Hunter College, African American male students have explained to the rest of us the daily offenses they receive from people passing by. Marc, for example, recounted how he is constantly followed by a sales clerk when he is in a store. The assumption is that because he is a Black male, he is there not to buy but to steal. Robert, a 6'3", African American student represented to the class—in a dramatic way that made us burst into laughter—the way people react to him when he enters an elevator or passes by. "People look at me and their faces go OOOOOH!" [opening his eyes widely and covering his wide-open mouth with his two hands]. Although we laughed at Robert's theatrical representation, the reality is far from comic. The multitude of offenses that Black males receive every day from all of us must impose an enormous burden upon their lives.

These stereotypes of Black males were expressed not only by the white women in this study but by the women of color as well. Francisca, a dark-skinned Latina, said, "I am afraid of Black and Hispanic people and they are my people." African American women described similar feelings. For example, Patty, one of the participants in a discussion group of Black women, shared with the group in a lowered voice:

I feel ashamed by saying this, but the image that comes to my mind when I think about criminals is that of a brother.

The rest of the group agreed with Patty. One of them, Pilar, claimed that the reason they all shared the same perception was that "we have all been raised in a racist society and we all have been influenced by the media."

The reality is that Black males are overrepresented in every area of the criminal justice system. According to a recent study by the Sentencing Project, in 1995 the criminal justice system held 827,440 Black men in their twenties, or 32.2 percent of all Black males in that age group (Butterfield 1995, A-18). Contrary to what some may believe, however, more whites are *arrested* than Blacks. For example, of all persons arrested in 1993, 7,855,287 were white and 3,647,174 were Black (Bureau of Justice Statistics 1994b, 388). According to Michael Tonry, Professor of Law at the University of Minnesota and author of the book *Malign Neglect: Race, Crime and Punishment in America* (1995), since the 1970s Blacks have accounted for approximately 45 percent of those arrested for violent offenses such as murder, robbery, rape, and assault. Yet Blacks are seven times more likely to go to prison than whites. Tonry (1995) identifies several reasons for the overrepresentation of Black males in the criminal justice system: the impact of the war on drugs on African Americans; laws that tend to punish Blacks and other poor minorities; and police activity, which focuses predominantly on the inner cities.

Cornie, a twenty-six-year-old college student, vividly recounted to a group of African American students what happened in the aftermath of a shooting on the Long Island Railroad. Her story exemplifies the consequences of media portrayals of Black men as savages and inhuman animals.

You know . . . I am talking about what happened in the Long Island Railroad with . . . what is his name?. . . Colin Ferguson. The image that the media presented is that he is an animal, a monster. . . . The next day I took the same train. You should have seen how people were looking at each other very strangely, in fear. . . . You know that they were reading about it; you know that they are conversing about it. People in their coffee shops were talking about it. . . . Everybody was talking about it. But, it was like . . . a racial division. In my school, the white professors, they were in their coffee shops talking about it. It affected them in a certain way. And it affected me and my friends who are Black in a different way. It was very strange. . . . The day it happened I read the whole story and I thought . . . oh God! Now every time a Black person enters in the damn trains all the whites are going to go OOOOOOOHHHHHH! Here we go again! This crime was horrendous, and yes, Ferguson is a Black man. But the way the media presented it was something that separated the races.

Millie, an African American teenager, expressed her belief that Black men are overrepresented in prison because of the fear they provoke. She said, "If we see a white male, we think there is nothing to be afraid of." Black males, on the other hand, provoke fear in the public as well as in the police, especially if they are together in a group. In her view, Black men join gangs because of their own fear, which in turn provokes more fear among people and police, who are more likely to arrest them. If a Black man "wants to smoke and needs to go outside," Millie said, "he gotta watch out for the cops and for the people who are scared of him."

Criminals as Animals

Criminals have historically been depicted and are still portrayed by the media and in popular discourse as animals or savages. Moreover, images of offenders as prehuman have been a persistent theme in the criminological literature. For example, the concept of the "atavistic" criminal has been part of biosocial theories of crime since the birth of criminology as a scientific discipline. According to Cesare Lombroso, the "father of criminology," there are three major classes of criminals: first, *born criminals*, who have reverted to primitive or lower evolutionary forms; second, *insane criminals* affected by mental illness, alcoholism, hysteria, and epilepsy, among other disorders; and finally, *criminaloids*, whose mental or emotional makeup could lead them into vicious, abhorrent crimes (quoted in Vold and Bernard 1986, 38). These antiquated theories have proved unscientific: the findings of the studies based on these theories have been unsubstantiated and have numerous methodological problems. For example, they rely on biased samples, such as people who are in prisons, as a representation of criminals. Nonetheless, these theories have had a profound influence on criminology and have helped to shape public discourse about crime, the creation of the outlaw, and the fear he produces. They have passed on to us images of the criminal as savage, bestial, and psychotic.

On April 4, 1994, a northern New Jersey newspaper, *The Record*, reported an incident that occurred in Prince George, British Columbia. A woman, Madonna Kelly, said that Andrew Rose, the man charged with two second-degree murders in the deaths of two German tourists in 1983, knocked at the door of her trailer in the early hours of October 3 or 4. "He said that he just killed two people," she said. "The moon was full and he made a noise like a werewolf" ("Witness Says Suspect Howled like Werewolf," *The Record*, 22 April 1994, A-13). Stories about werewolves, Dracula, and even Frankenstein excite our fantasies precisely because they touch deep-seated notions of evil, crime, and their connection to animalistic, uncontrollable forces. As Cornie's words sharply reflected when she spoke of the aftermath of the Long Island Railroad shootings, the role of the media in constructing "the meaning of crime and punishment in everyday life and popular culture" cannot be underestimated (Barak 1994a). This "mass reality of crime" has contributed to the construction of certain unquestioned assumptions about crime and criminals (Barak 1994a, 34). Animalized, racialized, and class-based images of criminals are important components of these assumptions. As Gregg Barak (1994a) maintains, with very few exceptions, the working class has almost disappeared from the world of commercials and TV programs. Consequently, there are three "media-created classes": the rich, middle, and criminal classes. The latter is consistently presented as out of control, undisciplined, lacking basic human qualities, different from "us."

The participants' responses reflect these images. When I asked them what images came to their mind when I said the word *criminal*, a large number of the participants shared stories containing images of criminals as monsters, savages, and prehuman creatures. In the words of Toni, an elderly white woman who lives in the suburbs:

To me, the image of a criminal is that man . . . that monster, who shot all those people on the train and then made his own defense.

Toni's words were followed by comments from Rose, another elderly white woman who participated in the same focus group:

That is the most scary thing of all. . . . Because you know that people like Ferguson are mentally unbalanced and people on drugs are also mentally unbalanced. . . . Most criminals are unbalanced. There is no way that you can reach at them. . . . When the people are mentally disturbed, they do not know what they are doing.

Several images are present in Toni's and Rose's words. One is that criminals are insane or unbalanced. This was a very common theme among the participants. On many occasions similar words were used to describe criminals: "crazy," "insane," "mad," "maniac," "nuts," "cracked," "bizarre," "weird." Also, criminals are out of control; you cannot "reach at them" or protect yourself against them. In other words, there is nothing you can do. The victim is completely helpless and at the mercy of these "mentally disturbed" men—a very frightening thought, indeed. Furthermore, the example that Toni and Rose used was one of a mass murderer, Colin Ferguson. This image contrasts with the reality of crime. Criminal statistics show that mass murders such as the one committed by Colin Ferguson, although gruesome and frightful crimes, are extremely rare. When these events occur, however, the media bombard us with reports. Politicians often exploit the moral panic that such frightening incidents provoke by promising us that if we will only elect them or support their programs, such incidents will be prevented.

In a similar vein, close to twenty of the women interviewed mentioned that for them the representation of a criminal was a serial killer, such as Jeffrey Dahmer. Gloria, a thirty-year-old African American woman, said:

You know, that monster. . . . What is his name? The one that killed and ate the hearts of his victims. . . . He was recently killed in prison. . . . Jeffrey Dahmer. Isn't that his name? He is for me a criminal, an animal.

Although Jeffrey Dahmer was white and Ferguson is Black, they share a similar quality: they are both seen as monsters, prehuman, or

atavistic, in Lombrosian terms; and Jeffrey Dahmer is the first image
that comes to mind when Gloria thinks about a criminal. Two criminologists, James A. Fox and Jack Levin (1994), disagree with the notion of serial killers and mass murderers as animalistic monsters. Furthermore, they dispute the belief that all mass murderers and serial
killers have biological or mental problems. In their view, these types
of criminals exhibit a sociopathic personality. Mass murderers, particularly, are often ordinary people driven to extreme acts by long-term
frustration or by other catastrophic loss—such as the sudden loss of
employment.

A related theme expressed in the interviews was that crimes are
committed during a violent outburst or a moment of insanity by, for
example, strange men on drugs or alcoholics wandering the streets of
the city. Some of the participants also described criminals as hanging
around with other criminals or "in bunches," as Isabel, an elderly
Latina woman who lives in lower Manhattan, said. "Ten, twenty, thirty,
they are always together." "Yes, like in a pack," another elderly Latina
responded. This representation is closely linked to the idea of criminals as animals. During the aftermath of the Central Park jogger's
rape and beating, some newspapers used this racialized, class-based,
and urban-linked image, describing the teenagers who attacked the
jogger as a "pack of wolves." Several of the participants mentioned
being afraid of Black and Latino teenagers who dress as "gangstas"
and hang around in groups. This representation of teenage "criminals" is yet another piece in the mosaic of fear.

Dehumanized Criminals

Leida, a thirty-year-old Latina participant, connected the word *criminal*
to *una persona mala* (a bad person) or someone *a quien no le importa
nada ni nadie* (who does not care about anything or anyone). Other
women used similar expressions, reflecting the common theme that
criminals lack human sentiments and are therefore cruel, inhuman, im-
moral, and evil individuals. These oversimplified ideas about good and
bad eventually become embedded in our conscious and unconscious
minds, weaving a complicated tapestry of class, race, and gender into
the imagery of crime. Working-class, immigrant, dark-skinned male

criminals are seen as evil monsters, animals prowling the night, waiting for their prey, the innocent victim: usually a child or a middle-class white woman.

These ideas do not occur in isolation. The relationship of blackness or darkness to evil has been a common theme in Western civilization for many centuries. Religious images are particularly striking and powerful: Lucifer is a dark male who personifies the forces of evil. God is represented mainly as a white—good—male who personifies benevolence. The influences that these representations exert on our lives are enormous. Growing up in a Catholic family, I can recall how, as a very religious girl, I pictured good and bad. For example, confessing and receiving communion had the power to—literally—wash out from my soul all sins, which were represented in my young mind as black spots. Sins were black; virtue was white. These connections do not stop with our religious images. On the contrary, they are transferred to many other areas of our lives. Because crime relates closely to issues of morality and sinfulness, its representations involve profound associations between badness and darkness, goodness and whiteness.

In the realm of criminology, these ideas found expression in the work of Raffaelo Garofalo, a positivist contemporary of Lombroso. Garofalo (1914, 33) attempted to develop a sociological definition of crime, taking into consideration "those acts which no civilized society can refuse to recognize as criminal and repress by means of punishment." These acts, he claimed, are "natural crimes" because they violate two basic human sentiments: probity and pity. Following Darwinian evolutionary theory, Garofalo claimed that criminals are moral degenerates who lack altruistic sentiments. He argued that society must eliminate those who are not adapted to the demands of a civilized society by three means: First, death for those who have such severe psychological and moral anomalies that they cannot live normal lives; second, partial elimination, including long-term or life imprisonment and transportation to colonies for those "fit only for the life of nomadic hordes or primitive tribes"; and third, enforced reparation for those who committed their crimes under exceptional circumstances that are not likely to be repeated. These ideas are not too far from the measures that sectors of the American public are demanding today: the death penalty, longer and tougher sentences for criminals, and deportation of illegal—or even legal—immigrants who commit crimes.

What We Believe about the Causes of Crime

As in other studies, participants believed that the causes of crime include a breakdown in the family or lack of family values, drugs, and a lenient criminal justice system (Skogan 1986, 170). Jennifer, one of the participants, said:

Everything goes back to the family. . . . You learn everything from your parents, from what they teach you. . . . But, if one of your parents is not there because . . . they are divorced or they have to work the whole day and the children are by themselves, you know . . . like watching TV the whole day and hanging out with bad influences, then you may easily do drugs and get involved in crime and end up in trouble with the police. Latchkey children. You know? That is a big part of the problem. These poor children come home and they don't have anyone to give them a warm meal.

Several important themes emerge from Jennifer's words. The first is the common assumption—especially favored by conservative ideologues—that children of divorced parents are more likely to become criminals than children of intact families. Fortunately, studies on the relationship between family structure and the onset of criminality discount such an association. They conclude that family discord is a more important determinant of behavior than family structure (Rosen and Nelson 1982, 126–135).

Second, Jennifer says that if both parents work, their children are in danger of becoming criminals. According to traditional roles, of course, fathers are supposed to work and mothers are supposed to stay home. It is therefore presumably the mother's responsibility, rather than the father's to ensure that the children do not "watch TV the whole day," do not become "latchkey children," do not "do drugs," and do not "get involved in crime." The fear that if something happens to their kids it is the mother's fault, as I mentioned previously, is present in many women's lives, limiting women's opportunities of work, education, and recreation.

Several participants mentioned drug addiction as a leading factor in driving people to steal or kill to buy drugs. Others referred to the effects of drugs on the individual psyche, making people "insane" or out of control. Victoria, an elderly white woman, said that people who are on drugs are "not with us. That is why they commit crime. If there is something that scares me it is someone that is not with us, someone on crack." Victoria's selection of crack as the drug most closely related to the commission of crime is not accidental. Unlike cocaine powder, which is an expensive drug, crack, a cheap, crystallized form of cocaine, is the drug of choice for people in the inner city. *Crack addict* is often a code term for a Black or Latino, poor, young, urban male (Goode and Ben-Yehuda 1994, 211–19).

Another common response of participants was to blame a criminal justice system that frees criminals before the completion of their sentences, "country club" prisons, violent juveniles who know that they can get away with their crimes because they are minors, and excessively short prison sentences for violent crimes. Women interviewed for this research shared various stories, including stories about women killed by men who had committed previous crimes, had been sentenced to prison, but were out on parole *à la* Willie Horton. Rosario and Blanca, two Latina women in their twenties, said:

Remember that woman that was killed when walking her dogs in Central Park? . . . Well, she was killed by a man who had been in prison and should have stayed in prison. But . . . they let him out . . . so he killed this poor woman. I guess he will be out again soon.

Yes, that is true. I know of another case of a woman in my neighborhood that was killed by a man who had been in prison. But, as they say, they get away with murder. He only served five years.

The conservative ideology about crime control, represented in the political arena by Newt Gingrich, Bob Dole, and other leading Republicans, and in the academic world by political scientist James Q. Wilson, has been incorporated into everyday discourse as an unquestioned truth. Such people advocate limiting the use of probation and parole, imposing the death penalty for a variety of crimes including drug dealing, and instituting longer and tougher prison sentences. The same attitudes were reflected in many of the participants, whose discourse mirrored the Republican agenda on crime control.

Notwithstanding the prevailing idea of prisons as deterrent, the reality is that they are not a very effective means to control crime. In *Power, Ideology and the War on Drugs: Nothing Succeeds Like Failure* (1992, 173), Christina Johns presents the twisted logic behind the argument that more prison construction will stop crime in a rather sarcastic way.

The logic behind prison construction and the continuation of the War on Drugs seems to be something like this: Prisons have been a failure, so more prisons will be a success; punishment has been a failure, so more punishment will be a success; criminalization and enforcement have been a failure, so more criminalization and enforcement will be a success.

Consistent with another popular theme currently favored by conservatives, some participants also referred to the violence portrayed by the mass media as a cause of crime. Bella, an elderly African American woman who lives in the suburbs of New York, said:

A lot of the time crime is from the television too. The television causes a lot of it. Because the television shows you even how they pick a lock on the door. . . . They have these crimes. . . . The television really makes a lot of the crime happen.

Other women in the group agreed: "Kids watch too much violence; so it becomes normal to them," Emma declared. Another participant in the same focus group mentioned the ownership of guns as one of the reasons people commit crime. "Before, boys would fist fight," Sylvia, a sixty-five-year-old African American woman, told the group. "Today they have guns and shoot each other. Guns and TV are a bad combination," she concluded.

Another underlying theme of the participants' narratives is that the root causes of crime are to be found within the individual. Most explanations focus on internal or individual sources of aggression and violence, ignoring the social, systemic violence that is constantly generated by patriarchal, classist, and racist structures of power. I am referring specifically to the violence implicit in an economic and political system that allows the rich to get richer and threatens more and more people with a jobless future. I am also referring to the violent acts that take place every day in the microcosm of millions of American homes, which are often dismissed as "private disputes."

White-collar, corporate, environmental, or government criminals were notably absent from participants' descriptions. Similarly, middle- or upper-class criminals who commit "street crimes" were completely excluded—with the exception of O.J. Simpson, who was mentioned by a couple of the white participants. Only one of the participants talked about organized crime, presenting it in a rather positive light. In contrast to the way in which films have dehumanized predatory criminals, organized crime figures have been humanized and even glamorized in movies such as *The Godfather.* Similarly, organized crime figures such as Al Capone and Lucky Luciano have been surrounded by a mythic aura that has converted them to quasi-heroic figures. We have been taught to admire them because of their intelligence, their enormous wealth, and their "values," such as love of family and community. Regina, an elderly white woman, said:

Several years ago, the Mafia even used to watch over us. Today, these criminals come from all sources of life. I don't trust anyone.

The contrast between this image and images of street criminals is unmistakable. The Mafia watches over us, whereas the almost mythical figure of the predatory individual lingers in the abandoned buildings and empty streets waiting for the next victim.

All these images present men as the main predators. "Definitely I am afraid of men," a student told me. "A man can overpower you," another young woman said to the group, "but I can beat up another woman." More recently, however, some women have also made it into the crime news. Susan Smith, the "monster mother," was cited by four of the participants as a good example of a criminal. Gaby, one of the Latina teenagers who participated in a focus group shared with the other participants: "If you leave me alone with her in this room I'll kill her. She is a monster." The media are increasingly exploiting the image of the "evil woman," although not to the same extent as men (Faith 1993, 257). But again, the main portrayal of Susan Smith is that of the abused woman who lost control and, instead of killing herself, in an impulsive gesture, jumped out of the car at the last minute.

Of all the possible angles from which the media could present the facts of a crime and the complex story of a criminal, only a few are chosen. Rather than presenting Susan Smith, for example, as a divorced mother who had to juggle work and child care responsibilities, the media chose to present her as an obsessed woman who saw her children as an impediment to her relationship with a man who was not her children's father. Smith's image as embraced by the media was that of an evil woman who slept with several men, including her stepfather, chose the love of a man over her children, and committed the most heinous crime that a mother can commit: killing her offspring.

The temptation to define criminals as bad, animalistic, and monstrous is indeed great for those who have been victims of crime or who have had to change their lives for fear of crime. The problem with cultural representations of criminals as dehumanized monsters, evil, animals, and the like is that they interpret crime as a personalized and private action, removing all responsibility from social forces that place extraordinary constraints upon some sectors of the population: unequal race and class relations, white chauvinism, and misogyny. Second, they dehumanize only those who commit street crimes, but not those who commit other, sometimes more pernicious, types of crimes. For example, those who engage in white-collar, corporate crimes, and state criminality were never mentioned by the participants as "bad," "monsters," or the like. It is as if the criminal behaviors of the elite are condoned and those of the lower classes, or the "dangerous classes," condemned. Some of the crimes committed by people in power, however, have enormous consequences for large sectors of the population: illnesses and loss of human lives in cases of pollution or unhealthy work environments; and economic losses in the cases of the savings and loan "scandal" (a code word for the crimes of the bourgeoisie). Third, most people who commit crimes are not "permanent" criminals. Many are also workers, fathers, brothers, husbands, boyfriends, or sons. For many people, criminal activity is one aspect of a more complex and intricate life. When we identify them as "permanent" monsters, evil creatures, animals, we simplify and trivialize the complex web of factors involved in the commission of a crime. Because crime is seen mainly in its moral dimension, it engenders an emotional reaction, rather than an impartial examination of the problem and a detached analysis of how to deal with it. In spite of the many criticisms of criminal justice agencies, the "answers" to crime continue to be more incarceration, tougher sentences, and even capital punishment. The growing fear of crime has helped to create an enormous bureaucratic apparatus intended to deter stereotyped violent predators. These continuously expanding bureaucratic agencies may make some feel a little better, but their effectiveness in controlling and deterring crime is highly debatable.

Criminal Acts as Random Encounters

Images of criminals imply that it is strangers who are most likely to do us harm. None of them reflect the reality of violent crime, in which most victims know the perpetrator. With very few exceptions, they do not depict husbands, boyfriends, lovers, or acquaintances as possible predators. Only some of the few women who reported having been victims of domestic violence said that the typical criminal was someone who abused his partner. "Criminals are inside of our homes," Lucia, a Hispanic victim of severe spousal abuse, said to me. In a passionate voice, she added:

They like to call them batterers . . . but to me they are the worst criminals. . . . Batterer does not have the same meaning as criminal, and that's what they are. . . . Once you have been in that situation, *Dios mio* [my God], you realize what a horrible crime this is. It is not a domestic problem; it is much more than that. . . . It is a real crime. Although society does not see it and likes to call it domestic violence, I call it the worst of the crimes and the worst criminals.

A Latina teenager, Mercedes, mother of a nine-month-old baby, also reported having been abused by her boyfriend. Like Lucia, she depicts him as a criminal:

I am afraid that he can take my son away. He is really bad . . . he is a criminal. . . . And he really can take the baby away from me. My mother has told me that he can hurt me badly. . . . And I went to the precinct to get an order of protection, but they didn't want to give me no order of protection. They did nothing, nothing. I went there with bruises, and they did nothing. . . . This man is really dangerous. . . . But they did nothing.

Evident in discourse about Sept 11

Most women, however, portray criminals as strangers. Thus criminals and noncriminals differ in nature, and probably in spirit, because they are "bad" and we are "good." This is an important aspect of the popular representation of criminals because it limits any kind of empathy that we may feel for people who commit crimes. Our only interest in criminals becomes to "lock them up" so "we" can be out of reach of "them." This attitude also leads us to believe, as one of the participants mentioned, that

Criminals have too many rights. Why are they going to have the same rights as us? We have not done anything wrong and they did. They took their chances and they should lose their rights.

The logic of this familiar argument is: If criminals are outlaws, animalistic strangers, why should they have the same prerogatives or privileges that we enjoy? In some cases, however, individuals change their minds as they, or a family member, become involved in crime, get arrested, and are sent to prison. Julienne, a nineteen-year-old, lower-middle-class white student, told me during our conversation:

You know, I used to think like most people . . . . You know, all that stuff . . . . Criminals are really bad people and the problem is that we are too easy on crime. Until the day my brother was arrested. You know, the judge didn't even consider that this was his first offense. I went to visit him. He is in Sing-Sing, you know, upstate New York. This was a shocking experience. I went with my mother. And we couldn't even touch him. He is in prison for drugs. And, don't get me wrong, I am not saying that what he did was right. But he is very young and naive. It may sound strange to you . . . but I know him well, and he is a wonderful guy [with tears in her eyes]. He was always very nice to me. He always has been my best friend. I cannot believe that he is in prison. I get so worried that he can get raped or killed. My mother is really depressed. Can you imagine? Her son in prison? This experience really made me change my mind. They really treat them badly.

Most of the images suggested by the participants are those of predatory, extremely violent, criminals who attack at random. These kinds of crimes, which dominate the mass media as well as political and public discourse, however, are the kinds that are least likely to occur. The distortion of the horror stories has trained us, especially women, to fear heinous, extremely violent crimes committed by strangers, which are quite rare occurrences. Sandra, a middle-class white junior college student shared with the group the horror story that is at the center of her fears:

My biggest fear is to be randomly taken away and my body to be found in a forest or in a ditch, you know, and have my family saying: "I thought she just went to the store, but she never returned." You know . . . that is really scary. I mean, the very thought that any time I am walking anywhere, and some lunatic can take control of you and kill you and end your life like that. And, many times they rape and torture you before killing you. . . . That is the worst.

When I asked Sandra, "How likely do you think that an incident like that can happen to you?" she responded, "I really do not know, but *it seems very real to me*" (her voice showed the emphasis).

A look at the statistics of arrests indicate that in 1993, of 2,848,400 people arrested for index crimes (those crimes considered most serious by the FBI), less then 30 percent were arrested for violent crimes. This means that 70 percent are *not* violent crimes but crimes against property (Bureau of Justice Statistics 1995a, 374). As Ray Surette indicates, "The crimes that dominate the public consciousness and policy debates are not common crimes but the rarest ones" (1994, 131). The infrequency of violent victimization notwithstanding, predatory strangers are a constant presence in our homes and lives through newspaper stories, TV dramas, films, and, very importantly, the nightly news. All these sources play their parts in constructing these "media icons" (Surette 1994) and thus reconstructing our own "reality of crime." As Sandra implied in her story, what is important is *what is real to me*, which is to say, my reconstructed reality.

The nightly news is especially significant in this reconstruction of reality. "If it is in the news, it should be true," Elba, a Hispanic teenager, told me. Advertisers understand this connection between "news" and "truth." I recently met a woman whose work is to sell space for TV to advertisers. During our informal conversation she mentioned that advertisers prefer to place their ads on a news program because this makes it sound more convincing. In the same manner, the daily news about crime has an aura of veracity: many of the participants used the sentence, "I saw it in the news" before or after recounting their anecdotes about crime as if to indicate that they were not discussing a fantasy or a story but information that is real—or true—because it was presented in the news.

Politicians also use media icons and horror stories—meaning bizarre acts committed by strangers—to frighten the public and to gain our support under the assumption that they are going to protect us by incarcerating criminals for life or, better still, by sending them to the electric chair or the gas chamber. The point is that this reconstructed reality becomes an incontrovertible truth, an "every-one-knows it" assertion, molding our fears and deep anxieties, shaping everyday public discourse, and influencing political decisions that affect the lives of millions of human beings.

Chapter Six

Coping with Fear

After I saw on TV what they did to that woman . . . the one
that was raped in Central Park . . . the jogger. . . . If you
don't protect yourself. . . . Well, I have unfortunately decided that I am going to shoot them so dead they won't get
up. So, I walk around with a gun.

> Jan, a twenty-nine-year-old white
> schoolteacher who lives on the Upper
> East Side of Manhattan

The entire criminal justice system has failed. And you and
I are paying the price in the lack of personal security because the criminals no longer fear the system. So, I have to
protect myself. . . . No one else is going to do it. . . . I carry
Mace. I don't take chances. I work night shifts and come
home very late.

> Heather, a thirty-two-year-old African
> American nurse who lives in Brooklyn,
> New York

For my last birthday, Juan, my boyfriend, gave me a beeper.
I like it because now he and my mother can reach me all
the time and this makes me . . . and them feel safer. I would
like to have a cellular telephone, but they are too expensive.

> Carmela, a twenty-one-year-old Latina
> student who lives in Queens, New York

Women's responses to fear of crime are varied: some lock themselves
within the invisible or, oftentimes, tangible walls of their apartments,
houses, or nursing homes, constraining their lives considerably. Others
develop protection rituals that allow them to continue with their lives
without consuming too much of their time or energy worrying about
crime. Still others respond by "not letting fear control my life" or by
carrying forms of protection such as Mace or pepper spray, or even a
weapon such as a knife, a scissors, or a gun. This chapter focuses on

the following questions: How do participants commonly respond to the possibility of becoming the victim of a crime? Are their responses mediated by age, race, and socioeconomic background? What protection rituals do women most commonly employ to manage their fears? Do these rituals reinforce gender-based relations? Do women feel protected by the agencies of the criminal justice system, specifically by the police?

Women respond to their fears of victimization in a variety of ways. Some of their responses may seem acquiescent, submissive, and even passive to us: locking themselves inside their homes, avoiding certain streets and activities, refraining from civic or religious activities. Others may seem more assertive and forceful, showing the women's determination to continue with their lives and not allow their fears to dictate their behavior. Some coping strategies may seem to reinforce the gender patterns of protected/protector or weak/strong, while others may challenge such patterns. Some strategies reveal a great deal of resourcefulness—as well as significant dissatisfaction with the social situation that constrains women's lives. Most women have to spend a great amount of energy, time, and economic resources to shield themselves from criminal victimization and to minimize their fears: take a cab; buy Mace; purchase alarms, locks, Clubs, or other devices; spend money in parking garages; and walk on streets that take them out of their way. Although men also have to take some precautions, studies show that women employ more avoidance strategies (Stanko 1990, 14).

Michel de Certeau mentions how "the act of walking is to the urban system what speech is to language" (1984, 97). Walking through a city has several functions, says de Certeau: (1) the appropriation of certain streets or places by individuals, similar to the appropriation of language by the speaker; (2) the spatial acting-out of the place by individual actors, as speech becomes an acting-out of language; (3) the creation of relations among different actors in that particular space and among that unique place and other areas of the city, just as speech establishes relations between the speaker and the interlocutor (de Certeau 1984, 97–8). The process of choosing certain streets and not others reinforces the assumptions that certain places should be avoided and others should be sought out as "inviting." In urban centers, "inviting" places are normally those with beautiful or charming stores—which sell clothes and commodities that most of us cannot afford—and those with middle- or upper-class homes and neat lawns. As individuals walk through these places and not others, they are, through their presence, making the place safer from crime and reinforcing class hierarchies in the urban space. By avoiding of certain places, they are buttressing the belief that poor neighborhoods are dangerous and should be circumvented.

Many of the participants in this research gave clear indications of the personal maps they create as they walk through the city, especially in New York City and the surrounding boroughs. "I never walk down [name of the street]," or "I don't go to [name of a certain neighborhood]," were common expressions. And the places commonly avoided were lower-class, predominantly Black and Latino, areas.

In discussing their different strategies, some women at first said that they did not do too much to protect themselves, because "I am not really afraid," while in the next sentence, they shared the different manners in which they respond to the fear in their lives. In focus groups, some participants pointed out to other members of the group the conflicting nature of these assertions. But what becomes evident in such contradictory statements is the emotional nature of the fear of crime. By emotional I do not mean, as other authors have suggested, that fear of crime is irrational or unrealistic. On the contrary, the fear of crime is a response to threats and criminal incidents that many women and their relatives encounter daily at home, in the workplace, or on the streets. It is emotional, however, because the fear of crime encompasses a multitude of symbols, representations, and codes that go beyond the reality of crime and are embodied in the image of the faceless stranger and in the horror stories of abductions and decapitated female bodies.

Although a few women, especially elderly women, admit to limiting their lives to the extreme of becoming prisoners in their own homes, the majority deal with their fears in a less confining manner. Most women have developed their own protection rituals and regularly use more than one coping strategy to deal with their fears. Some women depicted these rituals as, "You know, I do the normal things that we all do." On many occasions, lower-class and minority women

expressed frustration at being forced by their circumstances to engage in activities that put them at risk, in spite of the perils to which
such activities expose them. Some must work night shifts and have no
other option but to take public transportation during late hours of the
evening. If they were given the choice, many of them would gladly
work day shifts or use a private vehicle. Other participants expressed
frustration at having to attend evening classes. However, they must
support themselves and their children and pay for their own education, so they have to work full-time. Some participants asserted that,
"If I could, I would like to move from this neighborhood to a better
area, but I can't afford it." Therefore, it became very clear throughout
the study that many of the rituals and the avoidance strategies used
by the participants are mediated by socioeconomic constraints.

Women's coping strategies are also mediated by physical constraints. The elderly and women with disabilities or health conditions
mentioned avoiding crowded places, public transportation, and night
activities more often than those who were physically fit. Terry, a forty-
three-year-old African American woman who is blind, reported such
an experience:

I need someone to take me out. Although I can go out by myself, the fear
that someone might try to mug me or rob me scares me to death. You hear so
many stories about blind people being pushed into the tracks or being
pushed down the stairs . . . for nothing. . . . I don't take no chances.

Several of the most common reactions to the fear of crime include
self-isolation, target hardening, altering personal appearance, looking
for guardians, ignoring fears, guarding one's children, carrying protection, and fighting back. Women commonly said that they use or
have used more than one of these strategies. Some of them expressed
anger and frustration for "having to live my life this way." Only a couple of participants in the study expressed the belief that the limitations that fear of victimization imposes upon their lives violate their
rights to the use of public space or to equal treatment in society. Carmen, a twenty-two-year-old Latina student, for example, said that the
fear of crime and the preventive actions that she has to take to avoid
being a victim are "a reminder of do's and do not's that our society imposes upon us as women. Men do not have to take the same precau-

tions." As she spoke, Carmen's voice reflected the irritation that she feels for having her life limited. Although only a very small number of women referred to the impact of fear of crime in legitimizing gender hierarchies, several were openly critical of the social atmosphere created by such fear and of the special burden that such fear imposes upon women. Some of their narratives reflected not only the manner in which these fears constrain their behaviors but also the belief that some women do consider this situation "unfair," *injusta* (unjust), or even *una discriminación* (discriminatory).

A Strategy of Self-Isolation

Studies show that women and the elderly are particularly likely to restrict their activities for fear of criminal victimization (Clemente and Kleiman 1977; Gordon and Riger 1991; Riger and Gordon 1981; Riger et al. 1978; Skogan 1987). In this research, although the use of isolation strategies such as staying inside the home and avoiding certain places were documented by most women regardless of their age, race, and socioeconomic background, some strategies were favored by certain groups of women. For example, elderly women avoided going out of their homes more often than younger women. Among elderly Latina women, especially, avoiding the streets almost entirely was a frequent strategy. During a focus group with these women, three of them, Beatriz, Lola, and Maga, discussed their strategies with a certain degree of sadness in their voices:

Yes, I am older and not as quick as I used to be. This fear, I know, has stopped me from enjoying my retirement. Last year I was mugged. . . . Now I stay in more often, almost all the time. *Me siento aislada y muy sola* [I feel isolated and very lonely]. . . . Thank God I have the soap operas to keep me company and my *novenas* [prayers].

I used to go to church, but now I don't even go to mass because I am afraid of walking the streets of this neighborhood. Even during Christmas. . . . I used to go to the midnight mass . . . I loved it. But in our church, they had to change the midnight mass on Christmas eve to 8:00 p.m. because people were afraid to go out that late. . . . You know, life is not the same.

Since I was robbed after cashing my social security check, I do not go out by myself anymore. I go out only if I have to, which is twice a month, at the most.

The increased life expectancy of people in this country has length-
ened their retirement years. Therefore, the quality of life of those
millions of Americans now in retirement is a matter of great importance for social research. The fear of crime, such as that expressed by
these three Latina women, clearly affects the quality of life of elderly
persons, contributing to their sense of isolation and loneliness. The
fact that women live longer than men makes it imperative to comprehend the way in which fear of crime restricts the behavior of elderly
women. Fátima, another elderly Latina woman, also shared with me
that she only goes to those places where she has to go and not to places
she wishes to go: she never takes a walk or goes out of her house unless she has "something to buy or something specific to do. I used to
go to the movies," she said, but "I don't go anymore because I am
afraid of being mugged. You know, I am old and if someone mugs me,
I could be hurt," she concluded. "Would you like to go out more
often?" I asked Fátima. "Of course," she emphatically declared. "But
I can't. I am just terrified of being mugged."

Although the elderly Latina women in the study were often constrained by their fears, there were some important exceptions. One
of them, Blanca, a seventy-five-year-old Latina woman whom I interviewed in a senior center in the Lower East Side of Manhattan, said
to me:

When my husband was alive I didn't go anywhere but only with him. I had to
wait until he came back home to go out. He did all the shopping. I didn't go
anywhere. He didn't allow me to go out by myself. He thought that he was
protecting me. He had a bad temper. . . . I was married for thirty-seven years
and I felt like a prisoner. Without lying to you, I can tell you that I spent months
without going out of the house. Nothing, nothing. I was at home all the time
listening to music or reading or weaving or doing a little something. My husband died eight years ago and one week later I decided to take to the streets. I
would leave the house and not even cook. . . . I would take money and eat in
restaurants. And I went to the parks. Even during the winter I am out in the
parks, sitting in a bench. I didn't know anyone before. Now everybody knows
me. I am not afraid any longer. . . . I stay in the park until I want: Until 1:00,
2:00, 3:00, 4:00, and then at 5:00 A.M. I go upstairs to my apartment. If the elevator doesn't work, I take the stairs. I live in the ninth floor. . . . Because I
thought. . . . well, I have to live my life now and I have to protect myself. Do
you understand?

Blanca told me about several incidents and about the different methods she learned of protecting herself. Her story is particularly appealing because it illustrates the case of an elderly woman who became independent after her abusive husband died. She felt that she had freed herself from the prison in which she lived for thirty-seven years. She had to wait, however, until her husband died. Blanca shared with me her belief that her husband "made her weak." "When he was alive," she said, "I was always terrified. Now I am not afraid," she concluded.

Among elderly white women who live in the suburbs, the situation is less restrictive than for other elderly women because they have private automobiles and can drive to certain "safe" places where they feel less vulnerable. Nevertheless, one of them commented, "I only go out during the day." Two of them, Rose and Norma, engaged in the following conversation:

If I want to go for a walk, I only go to the malls. That is the only place where I walk. There is a lot of security there. . . . And I do not take anything with me. Only my car keys. That's all I take.

I used to be an outdoor person. . . . I love nature, and I used to go for walks in the woods. But there is no way I would do something like that now. . . . Besides, my children would think that I am crazy. Why worry them?

Some elderly women are strongly influenced by the fear of crime in deciding where to live. Elizabeth, a seventy-five-year-old, working-class Jewish woman, said that she used to live by herself. Her own fear of being a victim and her family's worries led her to move into a nursing home, "to be safer. Although I really enjoyed very much living by myself."

A large number of participants said that they avoid certain areas of the city. These areas are not always those with high crime rates, or even those that are believed to be dangerous, but rather those that are unfamiliar to them. Some women who live in Manhattan's public housing, for example, said that they would never go to Brooklyn, and some women living in Brooklyn said that they would avoid going to Manhattan. One woman who lives in an area of Brooklyn often considered unsafe emphatically declared that "Manhattan is too dangerous." These findings are consistent with Mark Warr's (1990) study,

which documents the relationship between fear of crime and the unknown. Using data from a mail survey conducted in Dallas, Warr
found that unfamiliar environments are more likely to produce fear of
criminal victimization than familiar places.

Other women avoid going out in the evening or avoid engaging in
night activities. For example, some react to their fears by restricting
their leisure activities. A group of Latina teenagers said that they no
longer go dancing, because they are afraid. Some teenagers said that
they have restricted their participation in sports and after-school activities out of fear of crime. "I love to play basketball," one of them
said. "But I can't because the practice is during the evening and I
don't have a ride home."

Studies show that women's control of leisure is not merely a matter
of personal enjoyment and gratification, it is "an integral part of social
relations" (Green et al. 1991, 78). Leisure is necessary not only for
physical, mental, and spiritual well-being but also for the formation of
social networks, which are fundamental to the social and professional
advancement of individuals. Social contacts initiated during leisure
activities—sports, dinners, parties, and other forms of recreation—
become important sources of information on educational and career
opportunities. For those with limited social networks, these contacts
are restricted. Thus women's lower rate of participation in leisure activities has a profound influence on their lives. Such activities are to
some degree constrained by men's control of the economic resources
within the family, as studies have shown (Green et al. 1991, 78). Few
researchers have focused on the control that fear of crime imposes on
leisure and the impact of this control on the quality of life and opportunities for development of millions of women. Some studies indicate
that women's participation in activities outside of the home are lower
than men (Green et al. 1991, 77). Indeed, as some of the interviewees
in this study reveal, one factor contributing to women's lower rates of
participation in leisure activities is their own or their families' fear of
criminal victimization.

Other forms of self-isolation include walking fast and "shutting
everyone out." "I just walk and do not look at anyone's eyes. If someone tries to talk to me, I just ignore him." This attitude, considered
commonplace among people in large cities such as New York, was

used by many women as a means of protection. Even though this reaction is comprehensible given the sexual harassment that many
women face on the streets, it also has some detrimental consequences. For example, it contributes to decreased social solidarity
among people by severely constraining personal interaction. Several
women reported that they refuse to help someone in need of assistance because of their fear of victimization. "If someone asks me for
directions, I just walk away. You take a big chance if you try to help,"
an elderly white woman reported. Edith, an elderly Latina woman,
used this interesting phrase: *el que se mete a redentor sale crucifi-
cado* (whoever pretends to be the Redeemer, dies crucified). Edith's
words mean that the person who tries to do good by helping others
easily ends up being hurt. This type of attitude certainly contributes
to individual cynicism, lack of cooperation, and decreased social solidarity.

Several of the women interviewed, especially those who live in New
York City, mentioned that they "walk with an attitude," so people do
not "mess with me." One twenty-seven-year-old African American
woman said:

Often strangers, and even my friends wonder why I constantly possess a
tough attitude. I feel that if I act "tough," like a man is supposed to act, I feel
the harm will not come to me.

In a similar vein, Josephine, a middle-class white woman, said that
the way she protects herself is:

Basically, I shut everyone down. I walk quickly on the street, don't look anyone in the eye, but I am aware of my surroundings and I have an attitude.

Another consequence of women's self-isolation is a decrease in the
use of informal social control mechanisms. Some women said that
they avoided attempting to stop deviant or criminal incidents, even
though they believed they could have been successful. In this way,
fear of crime helps to increase crime by reducing the informal social
control that noncriminal or nondeviant individuals exercise on others.
Law-abiding citizens may be afraid to intervene in potentially threatening situations for fear of being harmed. Joyce, a middle-class white
woman in her early thirties, recounted:

One day, while I was coming home, I saw a young man trying to steal some-one's radio from their car. . . . When I saw him trying to break into the car I tried not to look at him. . . . I did not want him to see me looking because if he gets arrested he might think that I was the one that told the police. My fear of being a victim in my own neighborhood prevented me from having an offender arrested.

"Fearing violence, most people ignore bad behavior and petty crime in public places," reported a February 1995 *New York Times* article. Of 100 people interviewed for the report, the majority said that they keep silent when facing incidents of social incivility. Although people called into question their sense of civic responsibility, the example that they give to children, and even their own courage, the majority of people interviewed declared that they do not inter-vene because of their fear of crime. Even some police officials inter-viewed for the article said that law enforcement "should be left to professionals" (Stewart 1995, 1, 10).

The article does not mention sexual harassment on the streets as one of the most common "incivil behaviors" confronted by women on the streets. But few people would intervene against harassers when they are molesting a woman, at least in part because of the fear of be-coming, themselves, a victim of the harasser. "I just thought, Why doesn't anyone say anything to him or do something?" one of the women interviewed said. She was followed several blocks by a ha-rasser yelling obscenities at her. "But no one did anything. People do not really care. Everyone just looks after themselves," she concluded with resentment in her voice.

Hardening the Target

"Hardening the target" means "crime-proofing" one's property, or at least making it more difficult for an offender to steal it (Clarke 1983). It involves securing homes, businesses, and vehicles and also guard-ing personal items such as wallets, purses, and jewelry. According to a National Crime Victimization Survey (NCVS), people take various measures to feel safer at home: installing alarms, window bars, and warning signs; keeping dogs; engraving valuables with an identifica-tion number; and participating in neighborhood watch programs

(Whitaker 1986). Most of the participants in this research said that they lock the doors and windows at home—"even during the summer," one of them said. Others buy special locks and alarm systems, lights, and timers; and install bars on their windows and doors in an attempt to build their cocoons of safety. Women use other measures to give the impression that someone is at home "protecting" them. During the discussion with a group of suburban white teenagers, the following exchange took place:

When I am alone I put up my radio and pretend that there are many people at home.

Or the TV.

I talk to myself.

The other day I was at home alone and someone called on the phone asking for my mother. I said . . . she is in the bathroom. No way I am going to tell them that I am alone [everyone laughed].

A white middle-class professional woman in her late fifties who lives alone in the suburbs near New York City said that the message recorded on her answering machine gives the impression that more than one person lives in the house. The message is, "I am sorry, *we* can't come to the telephone right now." (emphasis added).

Although the question of who was in charge of security at home was never asked, several women volunteered the information that the strategies for hardening the house as a target of crime were carried out by the males in the family. For example, Yolanda, a twenty-year-old Latina woman, said, "My father always locks the door and checks the windows." Similarly, Connie, a fourteen-year-old white teenager, reported, "My father installed a lock on my bedroom door, so I can lock myself in my room when nobody is at home." Even a few adult women reported similar behavior. Diana, a thirty-year-old white middle-class mother of two who lives in the suburbs, said:

Yes, my husband is the one that worries about installing locks and alarms. Every night, he goes around locking windows and doors. . . . Even the car. . . . I hadn't even thought about that. . . . It is funny! . . . He goes out every night and makes sure that my car is locked. . . . So, I don't worry. I know that he is going to do it.

Although some modern homes are supposedly established on a more egalitarian basis, the hierarchical system is still reinforced in many areas of domestic life. Barbara Ehrenreich and Deidre English point out that in the "Old Order," the traditional Victorian patriarchal system has been reinforced at different levels of organization and belief (1978, 7). The home is one of the most important places where patriarchy is established and reinforced: it is a man's castle. Therefore, he must ensure that it is safe. Many women have grown up with this image of their fathers securing the home.

Those women who have private cars use Clubs, alarm systems, and radios that can be removed from the car. Several of the participants who drive said that they always check the back seat to be sure that nobody is there. "Since I saw that movie . . . in which a woman is kidnapped and the man is hiding in the back of the car . . . I always check," Gina, a middle-class thirty-five-year-old white woman mentioned. "I am especially careful in the parking garages; anyone can walk there and hide inside of your car."

Among the most common target-hardening techniques reported by the participants in this research are hiding or not wearing their jewelry, holding their purses in a way that makes them more difficult to steal, hiding their money in their shoes or in their underwear, and not carrying cash or any property of value. For example, Angela, a twenty-three-year-old African American woman, said that she used to wear gold, but after being robbed she now wears only silver or fake jewelry. Some women said that they look for purses that are difficult to reach into, such as those that have a flap and a zipper. Frances, a middle-class white woman in her seventies, shared with the group:

Crime is always in my mind when I shop for a purse. I try to buy the ones with long straps, so I can carry them across my chest. I also see if they are easy to open by someone trying to rob you . . . like in a crowded place. That makes me feel that at least I have some control. . . . I like especially the ones that have a flap, because they are harder to be opened by someone trying to pull your wallet out of your purse.

Other women reported that during winter they keep their purses under their coats, so they become less visible. "I bought an extra-large coat," one of the participants said, "so my pocketbook fits under it." Other women do not carry handbags, but use only belts where they can keep their money, credit cards, and identification. Some students said that although they use their book bags, they keep their money in their pockets.

Some women's target-hardening strategies can be especially offensive to certain people. For example, one African American teenager reported:

You know, some white women are so afraid of Blacks that they grab their bags tightly when they see a Black or Latino passing them by.

"Are you talking about Black or Latino men or women?" I asked.

Both. I have had women crossing the streets when they see me approaching them. It makes me want to do something, so they can really say, "See, all Blacks are the same." No matter what you do, it is not going to change their minds one way or another. So, why bother?

Suge Knight, the twenty-nine-year-old CEO of a record company that specializes in gangsta rap by artists such as Snoop Doggy Dogg and Dr. Dre, explained in an interview published by the *New York Times Magazine* on 14 January 1996:

Treat me fair and I'll treat you fair. I stand up for right. I'm always 12 o'clock straight up as long as you are straight up with me. But if you mess with me or my people, you've got a problem. If I wanted to, I could really scare the hell out of you.

Alternatively stated, Black men know that they frighten many people.

Although Black men are certainly topmost among many people's fears, they are not the only intimidating group in today's society. The following conversation with a group of Latina teenagers in Manhattan reflects the way in which some middle- or upper-class white women react toward them:

You know, sometimes it is almost funny. When these rich women drive around this area, or get lost or . . . don't know their way around this neighborhood, or whatever . . . they look so fucking scared.

Yes, you see them in their big cars, Mercedes Benz or . . . something, looking at you as if they were in a zoo.

The other day, I saw this rich woman with a mink coat and all these jewelry, driving this expensive car. . . . I don't know what car it was. . . . You know . . . I

think she got out of the highway and she found herself in this neighborhood . . . or something. . . . I was just waiting for the light to change to cross
the street. . . . As soon as she saw me and my girlfriend, she rolled her windows up. . . . That bitch. . . . Do you know what I mean? I am poor, but I
am a decent person. . . . It made me so fucking mad. . . . Who does she
think she is?

   Clearly, target-hardening strategies are mediated by class, race,
and gender. Since it is more common for women to carry purses and
handbags and to wear jewelry, they are more likely to be victims of
crimes such as purse or chain snatching. Therefore, it becomes a
woman's individual responsibility to take care of herself. The underlying assumption is that if she exposes her jewelry or if her purse gets
stolen, it is her fault for not being careful enough.

   Moreover, although all women said that they feel threatened by Black
and Latino males, some of them also reported similar feelings when
they are in the presence of African American and Latina working-class
female teenagers. "Some of these girls are worse than men. They are
dangerous," Pamela, an elderly middle-class white woman reported.
"Some women are becoming like men . . . sometimes even worse," Rebecca, a middle-class thirty-two-year-old white woman reported.

   During the last few years media reports have presented an image
of teenage Black and Latina women as violent offenders and as gang
members. The public perception is that they are becoming more violent, more physical, and more "like men." According to the Bureau of
Justice Statistics, the number of women imprisoned tripled between
1980 and 1990 (Bureau of Justice Statistics 1991). In 1991, 61.4 percent of all women incarcerated in state institutions and 64.5 percent
of women in federal prisons were members of minority groups (American Correctional Association 1992). So, one could argue that fear of
Black and Latina women is somehow justified. A close look at the statistics, however, shows that the increase in women's imprisonment is
accounted for not by a rise in the number of arrests for violent crimes,
but by an increase in the number of nonviolent crimes such as
shoplifting, check forgery, welfare fraud, and substance abuse—drug-
related offenses like driving while intoxicated(Chesney-Lind 1995).
Moreover, in a study of the arrest data on women of color in California, Florida, and New York State (whose prisons, taken together, hold

more than 30 percent of all women prisoners in the country), Coramae Richey Mann found that drug violations and prostitution—not
violent or property crimes—are the most frequent causes of arrest for
African American women (1995). The most frequent cause of arrest
for Latinas was also public-order crime, with drug offenses being the
most common. Thus minority women are not becoming more violent,
rather they are being disproportionately affected by the law-and-
order policies of the 1990's, including mandatory sentencing laws and
"get tough on crime" policies regarding drug offenses (Chesney-Lind
1995).

Strategies of Disguise

Fear of crime also influences the way women dress because of the
fear of being robbed, sexually molested, or harassed in the streets.
Fashion designers, eager to sell their expensive dresses, are capitaliz-
ing on women's fear by introducing "comfort clothes and body armor
for an increasingly dangerous world." According to an April 8, 1995,
New York Times article, body protection was Donna Karan's theme in
one of her latest shows. "Men's suits, quilted jackets, coat dressing
that stays on all day long, layers of fabric covering the body, padding
along dresses and jackets." The idea in most American shows, according to the article, was "the need of a woman to feel safe in her clothes,
physically and emotionally." The designs favor a "uniform, the suit as
seen for years by the Japanese, by Wall Street, and now by women
who are wary of unwelcome attention" (Spindler 1995, 31). Since
most women obviously cannot afford Donna Karan's dresses, they are
designing their own armor to protect themselves against possible acts
of aggression.

A large number of the women interviewed shared with me the
many ways in which they alter their looks. In general, adult middle-
class white, Black, and Latina women, as well as white teenagers were
more likely to report changing their appearance than were African
American or Latina teenage women. Josephine, a twenty-three-year-
old middle-class white woman, recounted:

I work in a store that sells nice and expensive clothes. So, I have to dress
nicely. But, before I leave work, I change my clothes. I hide my jewelry inside

of my handbag, wear my raggy jeans and my sneakers, put my long hair up, wear a cap, so I don't call attention. . . . I don't dare to take the subway, a bus . . . or even a cab dressed in my nice clothes.

Marcia, a twenty-two-year-old Latina, shared with the group a story about the rather drastic measures taken by a friend who is very afraid of being raped:

My friend is really afraid of rape. She thinks that if she wears several pieces of underwear, it would be harder for the rapist to do something to her. So, she made these special panties for her and she wears two or three at a time.

According to Marcia, her friend feels that wearing these layers of underwear would give her time to yell or scream or do something to make the rapist leave her alone. Her strategy demonstrates the fact that she sees rape as an ever-present possibility in her life.

Some of the adult middle-class Latina women interviewed also reported changing the way they dress "to avoid problems." Leticia, a thirty-one-year-old Latina, said that she does not wear short skirts or makeup to avoid getting attention.

If I wear pants I wear them loose, so my butt does not show. Even in the summer, when it is hot, I wear a jacket so my breast does not show. You have to take care of yourself.

Cecilia, a white teenager, said that she has to wear baggy jeans, baggy tops, extra-large sweatshirts, "like the rappers," because she wants to avoid being harassed. "I cannot be myself," because if she dressed differently, then "I stand out and I would be harassed. So I wear things that do not stand out." Pier, a twenty-four-year-old white woman who likes to roller-skate in the streets of New York City, said that she feels safe at night because she wears a cap holding her hair up, black spandex pants, and a dark jacket, so nobody can tell if she is a woman or a man. In order to protect themselves against crime, then, women often feel that they must defend or hide their bodies and even masculinize themselves. Under a system of patriarchy, the body of a woman becomes the object of males' desires and fantasies. This view is periodically reinforced by the media in films, advertisements, TV programs, magazines, and even the daily news. The persistently reinforced myth is that men cannot resist their urges when they see a desirable woman. The counterpart to this myth, for many women, is that the female body is something that a man can have access to if he wishes. It becomes a commodity, something shameful or dangerous to reveal— therefore, it needs to be disguised. As a result, it is a woman's responsibility to take care of herself by dressing conservatively and by concealing her feminine features. "I wear clothes that don't show my body," was a common phrase used by many women, especially by white women and some of the middle-class Latinas. Many of them explained in detail the types of costumes they have to wear to camouflage their bodies, such as extra-large jackets, baggy pants, and oversized coats.

Carol Brooks Gardner (1995, 25) points out that "for women in public, crime prevention does not mean to refrain from pulling a bank heist or turning a mean penny as a pickpocket. For women, crime prevention is essentially, evading the role of a target for men criminals by muting personal attractiveness." As some feminist researchers have concluded, women's bodies are constantly defined as the property of men and therefore as vulnerable to unwanted male attacks (Radford 1991; Radford and Russell 1992). Thus many women find that one way to protect themselves against becoming a victim is to bury their bodies under an armor of oversized or masculinized pieces of clothing. Thus the motto becomes: "Good girls don't show their bodies, they dress decently."

Those who do not follow the dress code are demonized. In fact, during a discussion with a group of Latina teenagers, two of the participants, Marietta and Camille, conferred about the way they think a woman should dress:

I dress the way I want. That's nobody's problem. I even wear my gold. I love big earrings and gold chains.

We should be able to dress the way we want. . . . That is nobody's business. . . . If they think we look too sexy, that's their fucking problem, not mine.

Why is it that men can dress the way they want and women cannot? . . . I dress for myself, not for anyone else.

However, one of the participants, Mercedes, shared with the group how her own victimization made her change her mind:

You don't know what you are saying. . . . I used to think like you . . . I wear whatever I want and nobody messes with me. . . . That's the way I used to think . . . until I was robbed at gunpoint. . . . This guy put a gun to my head. . . . I thought that he was going to shoot me dead right there, . . . you know? I said shit . . . don't kill me . . . and he took all my gold. . . . Now I don't take no chances. I don't wear no gold.

During a discussion with a group of working-class African American teenagers, several of them said that, no matter what they wear, they are going to be blamed for their own victimization:

What I am saying is no matter what I do, they'll say, "Oh, look what happen to her, because her skirt was too short, that is why that girl was raped." We are not harming nobody, you know. . . . If I dress the way I want or go out at four o'clock, do that means that I am a hooker? Maybe I am coming from my girlfriend's party or something. . . . You know what I am saying?

So, there is nothing you can do, really, because whatever you wear they are going to blame you.

Yes, you know, Black women always get the worse.

And Black men too.

The attitude of these working-class Black and Latina teenagers reflects the belief that no matter how they behave or how they dress, they will be blamed for their own victimization—so, "Why bother?" Images of women of color, and particularly of African American women, have been "the focus of well-elaborated, strongly held, highly contested ideologies, concerning race, class, and gender" (Mullings 1994). A strong component of this ideology is an oversexualized and hormone-driven image of Black—and more recently Latina—women that has served to condone rape against women of color since the slave era. Even today, the rape of a woman of color, if ever reported by the media, is always considered "suspicious." These often discriminatory images, directed nowadays especially toward Black and Latina teenagers, serves to encourage conservative policies and campaigns, such as the ones aimed at forcing teenage mothers to live at home or risk being cut off from welfare, ignoring the fact that many pregnant teenagers come from violent family backgrounds (Males 1994). Since these teenagers understand the manner in which they are perceived by the wider, predominantly white society, and the difficulties they face in changing these perceptions, many of them have opted for acting "the way I want." Themes of African American and Latina teenagers as promiscuous and irresponsible welfare mothers burdening society and the welfare system divert attention from the role that social and economic forces play in severely limiting opportunities for poor teenagers of color, especially mothers and their children, such as restricted access to education, unaffordable child care, and lack of job-training opportunities.

Looking for Guardians

According to risk victimization theory, "All else equal, offenders prefer targets that are less well-guarded to those that are more well-guarded. Therefore, the greater the guardianship the less the risk of criminal victimization" (Cohen et al. 1981). One way that women prefer to deal with their fear of crime is by looking for guardians or protectors. In fact, many of the women interviewed said that they feel safe only in the company of others. For instance, some of the white and Latina teenagers reported that they do not go out unless they are in a group. Jody, a white teenager, said:

We always go out like . . . ten or twenty of us . . . you know, to the malls, or to skate. If I don't have someone, I stay home. It is too scary . . . and boring to go out without my friends.

Eugenia, a Latina teenager who lives in the suburbs of New Jersey, said that she and her friends don't go to the clubs unless there are twenty or thirty in the group. In her own words,

I don't dare to go by myself. Even when we go to parties we go in groups of like twenty or thirty or we meet at the party. I go to parties only if all my friends go. . . . I am afraid of people that I don't know. . . . And those who drive bring us home. If not I call mom. . . . Mom can you pick me up? [pretending to be talking over the telephone].

Although a handful of participants stated that it did not matter if the company was that of a man or a woman, the majority of them said that being with a man made them feel safer. After a discussion with the rest of the group, Eugenia concluded:

I rather have some boys in the group. . . . With boys you feel as if they are there to protect you. Like if they will prevent something from happening.

The most common protective figures mentioned by the participants were those considered "safe" men, such as husbands, fathers, boyfriends, and brothers (Stanko 1993, 132). For example, Maytena, a nineteen-year-old Latina student, said:

The main thing that helps me feel protected is my boyfriend. He is a 6'2" Black male and has a muscular body, you know. I feel that because he is Black nobody messes with him and when I am with him nobody messes with me.

Although many women said that they were afraid of Black males, several participants mentioned feeling protected when accompanied by their Black husbands, boyfriends, fathers, or brothers, including the white and Latina women who are involved in interracial relationships. Maytena knows well that to be with her boyfriend gives her protection because "nobody messes" with a tall Black man. However, she concluded, "I worry about him a lot. Since he is so big, people won't fight him. They'll just shoot him dead."

Similarly, white women mentioned that they felt safer when accompanied by their boyfriends. Josefa, a twenty-six-year-old white woman, said:

I have this sense of security when Russ, my boyfriend, is with me. It is like nothing will happen. . . . Ummm . . . probably what I feel is a false sense of security because if someone has a gun there is not too much that Russ can do to protect me. I do not like to feel that way, because it makes me feel dependent. You are always depending on other people, which is frustrating because I have always prided myself on being independent . . .

Some women feel that they need to be accompanied, even when they go to the bathroom. Two fifteen-year-old white high-school students, Adriana and Gloria, commented:

I am afraid of going to the bathroom in the school by myself. I always ask a friend to come with me and wait for me while I go to the bathroom.

Me too. Several girls have been molested when they are in the bathroom. . . . Some boys get into the bathroom and look at them while they are using the toilet. . . . I heard that one girl was raped in the bathroom of my school.

Several participants commented about having to depend on someone for protection. "My brother waits for me at the subway stop," Marlene, a nineteen-year-old Latina student said. "I have to call my father to pick me up," Audrey, a twenty-four-year-old African American student also said. Both of them expressed their dissatisfaction with their situations. According to Marlene, "It is a drag to have to depend on someone" [showing her discontent in her voice]. Fabia, a fifteen-year-old white woman, explained that her mother, who is a nurse and comes home very early in the morning, gets picked up by her grandfather. "How old is your grandfather?" I asked. She answered, "Eighty." This particular situation is an example of how, no matter their age, men are always seen as the protectors.

When women do not have live bodyguards available, some improvise. One of my students, a twenty-two-year-old white female, Natasha, told me that one of her friends, who commutes more than one hour between home and school, got an inflatable latex man that sits besides her in the car. "People believe that she is with a man and they leave her alone," she concluded. "She used to have a lot of problems. Her inflatable friend has stopped them," she concluded, laughing.

Others look for spiritual protection. Several of the women mentioned the fact that they pray to feel protected. A Latina woman in her forties shared with the group that she always carries her Bible. "So, I do not have to make eye contact with anyone's eyes . . . I always read my Bible, or pray, especially in the subway," she explained.

Even at home, women feel more protected when there is a male companion. Florence, a middle-class twenty-three-year-old white student, told me during an in-depth interview:

I used to live with four females and we were always scared that someone could break into our house. Now, we asked a male friend to move in. We all feel safer with him in the house.

With very few exceptions, working class Latina and African American teenagers were more likely than other groups to say that they can defend themselves better when they are by themselves. Phrases like "I know how to take care myself. I need no man to protect me," were more common among Black and Latina teenagers than among any other group of women. Mecha, a Latina teenager, mentioned that she actually feels safer when she is by herself because "I can run faster. If I am with other people I have to worry about them." Similar words were used by Cynthia, an eighteen-year-old African American teenager:

How can a man protect you? That's what they want women to think. . . . Oh, yea, sure. . . . Hey baby, I'll take care of you. . . . Sure. . . . The reality is that if someone has a gun. . . . How can they protect you? Sometimes they are the first to run . . . [laughing].

Women who had been abused by their partners also denied feeling more protected by a man's presence. Lucia, a twenty-five-year-old woman whose husband is currently in prison for abusing her, shared her experience:

It definitely makes me feel more secure to be with somebody. Not to be alone. . . . But I feel more secure with my mother, my sister . . . especially with my sister, because we are very close. My friend Sandy . . . I wish I can go out with her and feel safe. . . . But I will not feel safe once he comes out of prison. . . . And I do not feel safer with a man. He can be your abuser.

Although most women reported feeling safer when accompanied by a male, there were some exceptions. Some of the Black and Latina teenagers and women who had been abused by their partners reported feeling safer being by themselves or in company of a female friend or relative than when accompanied by a man. The difference between these and other women is that they know that their safety is not in the hands of a male because they have experienced or witnessed violence by those men that were supposed to be "safe."

Ignoring or Denying Fears

Of all the women participants in this research, teenagers were more likely to report that they ignore fears and continue with their lives. In one of the discussion groups with working-class Latina teenagers, I asked them, "What do you do with your fears? How do you react toward them?" The following conversation took place among four of them, Rosa, Daniela, Kathy, and Mercedes:

I bottle them up. Because I can do nothing about it.

The only thing I can do is to run.

I never think about them.

We should recognize that this fear is part of life . . . well I deal with it. Because if you are paranoid about it you will get nowhere with it. Deal with the fact that you are living in the ghetto, and this is not a nice place to be. . . . America made this ghetto for us in Manhattan . . . for us to grow up here and to fuck us up. Every city has its ghetto for poor people like us. . . . And they bring the drugs. . . . Then they say . . . oh, there is crime in that neighborhood. . . . They know it. . . . I deal with my fears by understanding that they want to keep us here. . . . I will leave as soon as I can and take my family with me. . . . And then just go on with my life.

Mercedes's narrative is especially striking for it reveals her belief that it is not her fault that she lives in the ghetto. She understands that she is there for a reason: because she is a poor Puerto Rican woman. She believes that "they know" that there are drugs and crime there but "they want to keep us here." "Who are they?" I asked her. "People who have power. You know; you are a professor: the government, rich people," she concluded, staring at me.

White teenagers also reported ignoring their fears:

I just don't think about it. You can't let it get to you. Things are going to happen good or bad and it just go day by day.

If you go . . . well, I don't think that I go to work today because I can get shot. . . . If you just don't go out, you may have missed something good.

Some of the educated adult white women also said that they don't let their fears control them—even when they have been harassed in the streets, mugged, had their bicycles stolen and their homes burglarized. "You have to keep working and living. What else?" one of them concluded, with an air of resignation in her voice.

Several adult women, regardless of their race, explained that they just ignore sexual harassers. Eve, a middle-class woman in her late thirties, said: "If you just ignore them . . . that is your best defense. . . . I just look somewhere else and keep walking." Only a handful of women mentioned that they disagree with this strategy, because they believe it is their responsibility to teach men how to behave toward women. These participants tended to adopt a political perspective on the roles of women and men in society. "They have to learn to respect women," an African American woman in her early forties emphatically concluded. Finally, a few women mentioned that they try to embarrass their harassers by thanking them. One working-class white woman in her early twenties said that when she responds to a harasser with a smile and a thank-you, "they get shocked because they do not expect you to act nice toward them. They want to scare you and you show them that they can't do it."

Guarding Their Children

Many American children live in a world of privilege, unknown to children in the poor nations of the globe. Some have access to state-of-the-art technology—the Internet, the World Wide Web, and electronic games—and a multitude of other forms of sports and entertainment. On the other hand, they see their lives severely restricted by their own or their parents' fear of crime. Children who live in poor housing units are taught how to jump into bathtubs to avoid stray bullets, and middle- and upper-class children are told how to scream when a stranger approaches them. Yet the fact is that of the almost 36 million children ages five to fourteen in 1991, only 519 were murdered (Adler 1994). In 1993 the rate of murder for children thirteen years and younger was only 2.1 per 100,000, compared to 12.1 for people fourteen to seventeen, 24.2 for those eighteen to twenty-five, and 9.1 for persons aged 25 and older (Bureau of Justice Statistics 1994b, 339). And many of these murders happen at the hands of parents or guardians.

Nevertheless, according to a recent *Newsweek*/Children's Defense Fund poll more than half of the children and 73 percent of the adults questioned expressed fear of violent crime against them or against a family member (Adler 1994). This fear is translated into specific parental behaviors: children are kept on a leash at the malls, alarms are installed on strollers, children are admonished not to talk to strangers, and many of them are being taught how to scream at the top of their lungs (Adler 1994).

Some of the white and Latina teenage girls interviewed were especially upset because of the restrictions that their parents impose upon many of their activities. During a focus group with white teenagers, which took place in the suburbs of New Jersey, the following conversation took place among Connie, Lynn, Jody, and Marilyn:

I am not allowed to walk outside of my house at night and I am not allowed to take the bus.

What makes me really mad is that my brother is allowed to go out whenever he wants. But because I am a woman. . . . It is just not fair.

I would like to go into the city a lot more. But the reputation of the city is that my parents wouldn't let me go in because it is like . . . you are going to get killed, you are going to get shot, someone is going to rape you.

My parents think that there are many bums walking there. I think they are funny.

I am not allowed to do a lot of things; my brother is, though. I am allowed to do some things, but if I need a ride home at night, I would not be allowed to go because my mom has to work or that type of thing. I am not allowed to walk home alone either.

Several of the mothers interviewed said that they do not let their children out of their houses by themselves. Some of them take very specific precautions. Tina, a twenty-seven-year-old Black woman, said "I had my children fingerprinted." Similarly, several white women discussed the way they deal with the fear that their children might be the victims of crime:

You definitely have to make your child fearful. . . . You have to scare them some. . . . You almost have to do it . . . because a trusting child is the one that is going to get hurt.

Which, if you think . . . it is a terrible thing to do to a child . . . but it is necessary.

But, I think that it is something that mothers have to do. . . . Middle-class kids are not necessarily safer anymore. Neither are kids from private schools. They even kick each other's faces in the bus.

This last participant's expressions reflect the fear in many middle-class homes that their class position is no longer a safeguard against crime. Despite this widespread belief, the reality is that are most of the victims of crime are still poor people and minorities. Socioeconomic advantages *are* a safeguard against crime. Media representations of random incidents of violence as if they were common reinforce the idea that we all have the same chances of victimization. This "democratization of crime" is just another illusion in the myriad of themes surrounding crime.

Carrying Protection

Several women in the study reported carrying a weapon or a sharp instrument to protect themselves and to feel safer. The devices mentioned range from beepers to Mace or pepper spray and from scissors to guns. Carmela, twenty-one, a working-class Latina student whose words were mentioned at the beginning of this chapter, reported that her boyfriend gave her a beeper as a birthday present to make her, himself, and her mother feel safer. Another student, Paulette, a white woman also in her early twenties, said that her father bought her Mace when "I told him that I was going to school in New York City." In both of these cases, as well as in others mentioned during the study, some women explained that men were the ones that bought the Mace, the pepper spray, or the beeper for them. Since men may not be there constantly to protect "their women," they are the ones that provide their daughters, wives, sisters, and girlfriends with something else to protect them, reinforcing the notion of men=protector/women=protected. In many ways, the perception of safety provided by the device becomes an extension of the father, brother, husband, or boyfriend's protection.

Some women explained that they use sharp instruments such as scissors, keys, and even rings. Carmen is a sixteen-year-old Latina high-school student who lives on the Upper West Side of Manhattan and seems very shy. She transforms herself as she begins to talk, especially when she shows me the two big sharp-pointed rings that she wears on her right hand.

There are not enough security guards in the high school. . . . I was almost raped by a teacher who had raped another student and had been in jail. If he approaches me again, I can hit him on the face right here . . . [pointing her fingers toward her forehead, between the eyes] in the eyes and blind him. He almost got me once. But I am ready for the next time that he or another dog wants to go for it.

Several participants said that they keep blunt instruments at home in easily accessible places. One Latina student said that she keeps a machete in her room. Similarly, Katheleen, an African American teenager who reported being abused by her mate, said that she keeps a baseball bat in her room "just in case that the asshole comes back."

An engaging conversation on the topic of carrying protection took place among a group of Latina teenagers. Almost at the end of the interview, after a good rapport had been built, they discussed the way they protect themselves:

I usually carry something on me.

Like a weapon or something.

I also carry a weapon with me . . . like keys or other sharp things to protect myself.

Come on! Tell her the truth.

Yes, I carry a knife.

And she carries a small gun.

"Do you think that you would use it?" I asked.

Yea. If I get robbed, it would take just one shot . . . bump! and that is it.

I don't carry a gun, but I carry something sharp, like a nail file.

A similar conversation took place among a group of African American teenagers:

I feel more protected with a gun; that is when I feel protected. . . . No man protects me. . . . They pretend to protect you and then they end up beating you up.

You know? That is funny. . . . I tell you something. . . . Me and my girlfriend, everywhere we used to go, we had to carry everything . . . a gun, a knife, or something. . . . But that makes you more scared. Do you know why? Because if someone fucks with you, you have no choice but to use that gun or let them hurt you. . . . If you are a happy person, you don't want to use that gun. . . . So, you are fucked up because you have the gun and you don't want to use it.

When you have a gun you have an attitude. . . . I am going to shoot them. I don't like that.

Gun ownership was also reported among a few of the white women, such as Jan, the twenty-nine-year-old teacher mentioned at the beginning of this chapter. A couple of them, however, said that their husbands are the ones that own the guns, "but they keep [them] at home," one of them concluded. Other middle-class white women also explained that they carry something sharp with them "like a small pocket knife" or "a scissors." Another woman said that she carries a whistle, "to call attention."

According to an article published in *Harper's Bazaar*, the gun industry and the National Rifle Association began to target potential women buyers when handgun production dropped from 2.6 million in 1982 to 1.4 million in 1986. Two appeals were used in the sales campaign: feminism and motherhood. Some images even depicted a woman with a gun tucking her children into bed! Colt Manufacturing Company published an ad in the July 1992 *Ladies' Home Journal,* instructing women to guard their children and themselves: "Self-protection is more than your right . . . it is your responsibility" (Horowitz 1994).

Fighting Back

Some parents are examining the crime statistics before choosing the college that their daughters will attend. "Before I came to this college," said Lillian, a middle-class woman who attends college in a small town in upstate New York, "my parents and I asked for the college's crime reports." Diane, another white college student, said "I wanted to go to another college, but it was in a bad section of the city, and my parents thought that it was too dangerous for me."

Several colleges and universities are now offering self-defense classes (McLarin 1994). Indeed, a handful of participants said that they had taken or were planning to take such classes. "I may not be able to protect myself if someone has a gun," Gwendolyn, a white student, said. "But I am sure it would make me feel stronger." Students who were involved in self-defense training mentioned that most of the instructors are males. "It is amazing," Gwendolyn said. "The self-defense class is for women but is given by males." Other students, such as Caro, a Latina teenager, take similar measures to protect themselves. "I am getting stronger by working out. I go to the gym everyday and do weights. It makes me feel stronger and safer."

Latina teenagers said that they form *gangas* (gangs) as a way to protect themselves. "We need each other," they said. "If not, other girls jump us." One of them said,

My girlfriends, are the only ones that I trust. They will go down for me. My friend Norma, for example, had three fights because of me, because . . . they will be like . . . they will look at me wrong . . . and she did not like the way they were looking at me. I don't let her fight when she is pregnant . . . I am like . . . you are not fighting with that baby.

We have fought other girls several times. We really care for each other. They are my real family.

Getting involved in gangs and/or in physical fights—a very "masculinized" response—was reported exclusively by the Black and Latina teenagers as a way to protect themselves. They feel that there is "nobody out there but my girlfriends."

The following discussion took place among a group of working-class African American teenagers:

I got a good story. . . . My mother used to go out every weekend, from Friday to Sunday and I had to babysit, and I was ten years old. I had to watch over my little brother and my little sister, who was ten months old. I used to be mad. But, now I feel that helped me . . . . First of all, I kept money in my pocket, because my mother used to pay me for that. Second, I know how to cook, how to do hairs, and I got to be more independent. . . . I also learned how to protect my little brother, my sister, and myself. And I grew up very strong and independent. . . . Now, white girls do not grow up that way.

Yes, growing up in the streets you learn to watch; you watch and you see the reaction of this person and that person . . . and you know that this reaction is not going to get you nowhere, and this reaction will get you somewhere. . . . So, it is like you are standing and standing; you watch what is going on and you just know right away.

See, a majority of white girls when they grow up they are into school buses or their moms drive them to school and they are not out there fighting, and if they don't fight, they cannot protect themselves. . . . You understand? But Black girls . . . they fight. . . . You know what I am saying?

I fight guys. If you fight with a guy you have to hit him really bad, because you know that you cannot beat them, so I try to toss something or to put a knife at him . . . because the man's body is stronger than yours.

White women have money to pay bodyguards or security guards . . . I am my own bodyguard.

(Laughter).

Likewise, a group of Latina teenagers discussed physical fights in the context of domestic violence. Three of them, Lizi, Ester, and Juana, talked in a very lively manner:

I think a woman who gets beat up in her home . . . that makes her stronger, so she can fight back.

This society does not do anything for you, like the law and stuff. . . . It is not going to get you out of trouble; they are going to lock him up for one day. Then he is going to come back and beat the shit out of you, because you called the police. . . . So you need to know how to fight back.

If he comes back and beats you up again, you need to be prepared with a bat or a pipe.

These women will become stronger and they will not take anything from another girl.

Working-class Black and Latina teenagers frequently expressed their belief that nobody is there to defend them. Thus they must learn to fight back. Most of them have lived their lives in a continuum of violence—sexual, physical, and psychological—at home and in the streets (Kelly 1991). They are clear about the fact that, for them, there are no "safe" men. Very early in their lives, they realize that they are responsible for their own protection and that there are no protectors. The only allies that they have, on occasion, are their girlfriends. Many of them believe—from experience—that they cannot count on the police. Indeed, if they turn to the police for their protection, they expect to encounter suspicion, mistrust, and further abuse.

Police Protection and Fear of Crime

The American public is constantly bombarded by media images of criminal justice agents as heroes pursuing and capturing criminals (Barak 1994). Additionally, many of the studies that show police helping to decrease the fear of crime (Balkin and Houlden 1983) do not control for the race of the respondent. One of the questions asked in the present study was, "Do you feel less afraid when the police are around?" The responses of participants differed sharply according to the race and socioeconomic class of the women. Whereas, with very few exceptions, middle-class white women reported feeling safer with a police presence, working-class Black and Latina women said that a police presence did not make them feel safer. On the contrary, most women of color felt intimidated by the police. During a focus group with Puerto Rican teenagers, the following conversation took place:

No way, when the police is around I am more afraid. I think, What are they going to do now? I am afraid of them.

They wouldn't do shit for you.

Most of the time they get there late, to the place where the incident happened. They don't know the story and they jump to conclusion that you killed the person.

The day they killed my brother . . . they got to the scene late, half an hour late. Right? The block was packed. . . . It was three o'clock in the afternoon. Then one cop asks first, then another, and they already are suspecting people. . . . When the man was arrested, I was in the police car. They drove me around so I can identify him. They were fucking putting me in danger, me and my family. . . . And then, in the funeral home the guys who killed my brother were shooting at my mother and at me. . . . They locked him up for a while. But now the guy who killed my brother is out. If my brother was white, that wouldn't happen, no way. . . . And if I was white they hadn't put me in fucking danger. The police say that he deserved it because he was a bad guy. I know that it is because he was a fucking Puerto Rican.

"How would you feel if the police officer were Puerto Rican?" I asked.

They are the same, or worse. They have to demonstrate to the others that they are tough.

Once my father was driving and we were stopped in the highway . . . with no reason. . . . It was a Puerto Rican and a white cop. . . . They were mean. . . . I was scared. . . . I think the Puerto Rican cop had to show to the white cop that he was tough with other Puerto Ricans.

María, a Dominican woman in her early forties, recounted similar experiences with the police. The way they reacted to her requests for assistance when she was beaten by her husband led her to believe that they would not help her if something happened.

It takes a long time for them to show up. When my husband beat me up, I called the police and when they arrived he was already gone. They wait until the last moment to do something and then it is too late.

Women of color often mentioned police prejudice toward Latinos and Blacks. "We cannot trust them," was a common answer. Many of them had stories of police brutality against someone they knew or had a story to tell about a personal incident with the police. "How can we trust them," a Black teenager said, "if they hate us?" Amaya, a Latina teenager, said that the police always try to protect themselves and their colleagues. Moreover, "they only protect the *Americanos*" [American people], she said. "If you are *Hispano*, you are going to be blamed, even if you are innocent." Another Latina woman in her thirties, Nancy, narrated a story in which a young Latino man was brutalized and beaten by the police because he asked an officer to stop harassing him. "The police threw him to the floor and beat him up with his stick only because he was Hispanic."

White women were more likely to say that they felt safer when the police were around. Doris, a middle-class white teenager who dresses conservatively, said "Yes, I feel safer when the police are around; they protect us." However, not all white teenagers shared her opinion. Indeed, the words of another woman, Carol, a nonconventional or "deviant" white teenager who, unlike Doris, dresses in a more "punk" style, reflect the differences in the responses that people get from the police based on their appearance. "I get harassed by the police all the time." Carol wears one nose ring and several earrings, dyes her hair dark black, and wears black leather pants and jacket. She also wears silver rings on every finger of both hands. "What about female police officers?" I asked her. "I hate women police officers," she answered. "I get harassed by one of them all the time at Washington Square."

One of the working-class white women who participated in an in-depth interview and who is the wife of a police officer, shared with me in a way that reflected the anguish that she feels:

I do not feel safer with the police. How can I? In fact, as you know, my husband is a police officer. Who do you call when your abuser is a police officer?

In conclusion, only adult and elderly middle-class white and Latina women and the more "conventional" white teenagers were likely to say that they felt safe in the presence of the police. "Of course, I feel safer when a police officer is around," was a much more common response among these groups than among middle- or working-class African American and working-class Latinas.

What Can Women Do?

One of the last questions asked of the participants was: "What do you recommend to other women to deal with their fear of crime?" The responses ranged from traditional measures that clearly enhance existing gender divisions to measures that challenge the status quo. Without a doubt, the most frequent responses reinforced traditional women's roles, confirming the major argument of this book: fear of crime helps reinforce gender hierarchies in U.S. society and organize consent about an appropriate code of behavior for women. The recommendations of María, a Dominican woman in her early forties, exemplify some of the most common answers:

Do not dress provocative, do not go out by yourself, do not go out during the night, but above all pray a lot and ask God for protection.

One Latina woman in her seventies, Ingrid, pointed out that women should avoid the streets "as much as they can." "It is not a matter of what I want to do. I really believe that I have no other choice, given the dangers out there."

Some women were especially emphatic when they urged other women to take responsibility for protecting their children. "Who is more responsible for protecting the children?" I asked Nancy, a thirty-two-year-old middle-class white woman:

Even if what I say irritates other women [she responded], the reality is that women are more responsible for the care of the kids, of course. That is the way it has always been and it has changed very little, in spite of women's liberation. Women still have more responsibility for the safety of the kids than men.

Although most of the advice was consistent with traditional roles, a few responses reflected a more politicized attitude toward fear of crime and its impact upon women's lives. Particularly relevant for this study was the response of Connie, a fourteen-year-old lower-middle-class white teenager, whose mother, Marilyn, is a student in a Women's Studies Program at a college in New York City. In a very clear and eloquent manner, Connie shared with me her views:

I am a woman and I can do something, instead of [raising the pitch of her voice] well, I need my husband to walk me down the street! Even if they need a can of Mace. I think women around the city and around the world should do something. . . . Have a protest. Say, look media, you have to project a better image of us because we are not wimps and we are not people who stay home and take care of children all the time. Not because that is a bad thing to do, but we are women who go out and make something of our lives. I think women should have a protest or boycott certain things. . . . Especially if they present a negative image of us. And girls should be educated more, such as math classes for girls so they think better of themselves. If they think better of themselves, they are more likely to protect themselves.

After she ended her eloquent message to women, I asked her, "What about men? Can they do something about fear of crime?" To which Connie responded:

Men do not want to do too much about the problem of fear of crime, because they are afraid of losing power because the media and other men are afraid of losing the power that they have. . . . They want to have that power because it benefits them. . . . So they do not care whether women are treated bad or not. Because if women do not work because they are afraid of crime, they are getting paid more in their jobs and all that.

Although Connie's words are not, by any means, representative of the views of the 140 women interviewed, they are important because they indicate that some women do understand how the fear of crime helps to establish and consolidate gender hierarchies. Undoubtedly, having a mother who is a student at a Women's Studies Program has contributed to Connie's consciousness of gender issues.

Although most of the strategies suggested were individual responses to the problem of fear of crime, a few women recommended more collective approaches. Illustrative of this trend was the response of some of the members of a focus group with immigrant Latina women, some of them undocumented:

The solution cannot be individual, because this is not an individual problem. Fear of crime is not your, or your, or your problem [pointing to the other women in the group]. This is our problem.

But you cannot go out always with the group.

No, I don't mean that. . . . For example, in the barrios in my country, there are meetings of the barrio, in which the families get together and we get to know each other. You begin to know each other and you begin to lose your fear. Now I know who my neighbor is. . . .That makes me feel safer.

Yes, here I don't even know my next-door neighbor.

One of the few women who disclosed that she had been the victim of domestic violence, Lucía, a twenty-five-year-old Latina woman, said:

I would recommend to women who are victims of domestic violence, especially to Latina women to fight against fear by swallowing their pride, if you have a family. You give up whatever you have, whether it is an apartment, whether it is furniture, whatever it is . . . a nice house, you give that up, because then you go somewhere where you feel safe. Give that up and go through the process. . . . Face your fears. It is a big step, because then you show them . . . I am not going to take this shit. . . . That is the only way to face your fears. Women should fight for affordable homes for them, so they can relocate. . . . They should have priority. . . . Not everyone, but those who qualify and have been involved in domestic violence should have priority.

Other women recommended coping strategies that are not consistent with traditional views. Among them are the suggestions of a group of working-class Latina teenagers:

I really believe that women should carry a weapon.

Women can beat somebody . . . a woman or a man. . . . A weapon puts us in an equal position to them.

"What if they also have a weapon?" I asked.

You can hit somebody and make them drop their weapon, and that is it. That makes men more mad. . . . Oh shit! . . . she was about to stab me . . . stupid bitch. . . . You know what I am saying.

[Laughs from the group]

Carry Mace but be ready to use it.

Watch for the cops.

Well, don't worry about the cops. . . . If something happens the cops will be the last to be there.

[More laughs from the group]

In brief, the measures that the participants recommended can be arranged along a continuum. At one extreme are strategies that reinforce traditional sex-role orientations: they accept the view that women are safer at home than on the streets, that women's predominant role is to protect children, and that there are "safe" men that can protect them. Most of the responses fall into this traditional category. At the other extreme are strategies that imply a more "proactive" attitude toward fear of crime and challenge conventional etiquettes regarding women's behavior. Such strategies range from becoming involved in physical fights to entirely rejecting the idea that there are proper behaviors for women.

Chapter Seven

Conclusions

Confronting Fears

A world without fear would be wonderful. . . . You know
that you wouldn't lose people that you love . . . or you would
lose them for natural causes . . . like cancer . . . and that
would be understandable. But how can you be happy being
afraid because your mother can be shot? I am afraid that
my sister can be in a car accident because my father is driving when he is drunk. . . . If there was no fear of crime, of
violence, of drugs, of alcohol, then I think I would be
happy. Yes, the world would be beautiful without fear of
crime.

I would feel free of going wherever I want . . . I would party
a lot [*laughing*].

People could go to their high school without fear of being
stabbed.

Like me, I am always afraid of being stabbed.

I would sleep in the park, looking at the stars.

> Focus group with Latina teenagers,
> New York City

One of the major purposes of this book has been to encourage readers
to be more critically aware of their beliefs and behaviors in confronting
fear of crime. I cannot teach women how to deal with their fears or
protect themselves against criminal victimization. Ultimately, every
woman must decide for herself how to manage her fears. But personal
decisions do not happen in a social and political vacuum. They are
strongly influenced by dominant ideologies regarding crime, criminals, and victims within a social context and social institutions that permanently reproduce relations of dominance and subordination.

151

Our everyday behaviors and fears support or challenge the assumptions about crime presented to us as unquestioned truths (Hall et al. 1978, 140), among them the simplistic assumption that women are weak and powerless, in need of protection, and men are strong and powerful, therefore the "natural" guardians of women. Living with these images confuses the imagined with the real and creates a society in which most people live according to the imagined. How we imagine crime (Young 1996) is shaped by representations of faceless strangers, maniacs, "weird looking," dark-skinned men who wait for their innocent victims in the dark alleys of the city, under their beds, or inside their closets. Such images persuade women to limit their behaviors and be "good" to avoid getting mugged, sexually harassed, raped, or killed.

The images that mold women's fear of crime and influence the way in which they face such fears are all a part of the dominant ideologies of crime. These ideologies are constructed not only by stories, conversations, and media representations of criminal incidents but also by stereotypical notions of criminals and victims. So frightening are these images that they have helped to create a strict code of behavior for women. The underlying message is that women who do not follow this code expose themselves to "unnecessary" risk; if they are victimized, it is their fault for transgressing stringent rules so ingrained in popular culture that "everybody knows them." Everybody knows, for example, that women should dress conservatively, should not be out in the streets at night, should avoid going to the "wrong" places and being with the "wrong" people, should not take jobs that expose them to danger, should be the primary guardians of their children, and should always be accompanied by someone, preferably a man. Thus the responsibility for preventing and controlling crime against women is placed squarely on the shoulders of women.

Women's responses to the fear of crime vary, for they are mediated by situational factors (Gardner 1995). As Richard Sparks points out (1992, 133), some people live in circumstances that force them into frightening social positions. Such social positions as being African American or Latina, immigrant and/or undocumented, poor, disabled, or lesbian or bisexual, play a role in the fear of crime. Immigrant women, for example, especially those who do not speak English flu-

[handwritten marginalia, left margin]: news articles about crimes against women reinforce this — always end w/ safety tips for women

ently or who are undocumented, have unique disadvantages when faced with the possibility of victimization. Their fears are mediated by images of not being able to understand the demands of their assailant or, if the assailant is a husband or boyfriend, of not being able to report the crime to the police for fear of deportation. Similarly, although women interviewed in this book were not asked and did not volunteer information about their sexual orientation, lesbians and bisexuals share with other women a sense of vulnerability in public places (Stanko 1990; Gardner 1995) and, if identified as such, may be harassed or even assaulted for being a threat to "traditional values." In fact, an analysis of the rates of criminal violence experienced by the entire population compared to homosexual men and women shows that acts of aggression against the latter group are much more common (Comstock 1991, 55).

The burden of crime falls heavily on women, but especially on women of color, who are more likely to be victimized than white women. Hearing their voices in the pages of this book is particularly meaningful, given that traditional studies on fear of crime have been silent about their specific needs. Similarly, teenage women's narratives proved especially significant, for their stories and testimonies have also been absent from most of the literature on fear of crime.

Some may argue that women can decide to defy social conventions, venturing into the world as, in fact, some do. But women do not independently *choose* either their fears or the mechanisms to cope with them. They do not freely *choose* to change their appearance to avoid being harassed in the streets. True, their decisions are individual, but such decisions take place *within the context of unequal power relations,* in which women know that men control the streets and that many feel they can harass a woman without any consequences. For women who are victims of domestic violence, the fear is exacerbated because their abuser is someone who is "supposed to protect me."

Studies on female fear of crime have focused predominantly on fear of rape and other violent crimes. Participants in this study, however, shared with each other and with me how incidents considered by many to be "less serious," such as purse snatching, mugging, offensive comments or touches in the street, at work, and in school, cause intimidation and fear. These incidents also make women feel powerless and dehumanized, treated as objects. The truth is that many women live in a continuous state of apprehension, unable to be sure whether or not one of these "small incidents" in the street or at home may escalate into a more threatening situation. A touch in the street may or may not become a sexual assault; an ignored comment from someone passing by may or may not become an insult or even a physical assault.

Reflections on Past Studies of Fear of Crime

Because most researchers have studied fear of crime within the context of conventional theories of crime and victims, they have ignored the structures of power that form the framework for criminal incidents and the fear that they provoke (Stanko 1991). The routine activity approach, for example, an important theoretical development in the field of criminology, focuses on the conditions that influence the likelihood of victimization. According to two of the proponents of this theory, Lawrence Cohen and Marcus Felson (1979), the risk of criminal victimization depends on those elements of life-style and routine activities that place people in contact with potential offenders, who in the absence of guardians gain access to their victims. Although studies based on this theory incorporate gender, race, and socioeconomic situation as individual variables, they view fear of crime as if it occurred in a social vacuum where power as a feature of interpersonal and structural relations is simply not an issue.

Skogan and Maxfield (1981) suggest that women's fear of crime is related to their social and physical vulnerability. In their view, social vulnerability is a combination of everyday exposure to the likelihood of victimization and limited resources for dealing with the consequences of a criminal attack. Physical vulnerability is a combination of the powerlessness to resist aggression and the emotional and physical consequences of victimization. Once more, fear of crime is treated as an individual or group characteristic. These studies do not even consider the constant abuses of power that women, people of color, and individuals with homosexual orientations experience every day.

This book views the fear of crime from the perspective of social constructionist and feminist theories. These approaches provide valu-

able insights and methodological directions for study. Social constructionism reminds us that our fears arise in response to images of criminals and victims (Christie 1986), and that these images mirror the
class, race, and gender arrangements of the larger society. The dominant conception of crime offers polarized images of ideal criminals
and innocent victims that galvanize public sentiments into an almost
universal view of crime and victimization. As participants in this research have shown, the dominant ideologies about crime and its control, criminals and victims, reinforce a vision of society in which Black
men are foremost among women's fears—regardless of the race of
the women—and women, particularly white women, are innocent victims of sexual attacks committed by strangers. The images that shape
these ideologies support the status quo since the prevailing social,
economic, and political conditions that help to produce violence and
fear are seldom, if ever, questioned, much less challenged (Barak
1994a). The imagination of crime helps to construct a "reality of common sense" (Berger and Luckman 1967, 10) regarding crime, criminals, and victims based on predatory acts committed by mentally
deranged or cruel individuals rather than on structural determinants,
such as economic inequality or power differentials.

Feminist theories remind us that the control of women takes a variety of forms, mostly outside of the formalized repression imposed
upon us by the agencies of criminal justice (Smart and Smart 1978,
1, 2). Instead of focusing on the more traditional question—"Why do
women commit crimes?"—some feminist studies of social control ask,
"Why do women conform?" (Carlen 1994, 138). I argue that fear of
crime is a fundamental element in the social control of women because it organizes consent around a strict code of behavior that "good
women" need to follow. As the voices of the participants in this study
demonstrate, with some important exceptions, most women adhere
to such a code. Although presented as individual decisions, the coercion imposed by the fear of crime upon women is structural, because
it is rooted in the multiple and overlapping hierarchies of power.

It is highly relevant to examine the roots of current crime ideologies and their function in promoting fear of crime. These ideologies
encourage such commonly held beliefs as: (1) criminals can be recognized by their physical characteristics; (2) crime and fear of crime can

be solved only by the efforts of law enforcement officials (Surette 1992); (3) Black and Latino young males and females and members of "new" immigrant groups form a dangerous class in the United States; (4) victims of crime are predominantly white; (5) it is the responsibility of women to avoid their own and their children's victimization by severely limiting their lives and in essence becoming their own police force; (6) "normal" criminality is the kind committed by stranger predators whereas crimes committed at home, work, or school are not "real crimes," because they are not committed by ideal criminals against innocent victims; (7) a woman alone is an easy target of stranger predators, so women need "safe" men to protect them because another woman who might come to her assistance will be of no help whatsoever (Brownmiller 1975); (8) if a woman does not have a protector, she should pretend to have one to be safe.

What to Do?

As a slogan printed on a t-shirt of the Taller Salud in San Juan, Puerto Rico, reads, *"Las niñas buenas van al cielo. Las demás vamos a todas partes."* [Good girls go to heaven. The rest of us go everywhere.]

I am frequently asked if there is any possible solution to the problem of women's fear of crime. The complexity of the phenomenon notwithstanding, I do believe that several approaches can effect individual changes and, eventually, gradual transformations in the larger society. Some of these suggestions deal with everyday actions and behaviors, and some are directed more specifically to the need for change in the broader structures of power.

Men's and women's seemingly innocuous everyday rituals of protection against fear of crime reproduce and maintain gender, race, and class stereotypes and expectations. Some of the participants in this study reported how offensive these rituals can be: for example, a woman rolling up her car windows when passing a group of Latina teenagers. Becoming aware of these seemingly innocuous rituals and of their effects on interpersonal relations and on the larger society cannot be overemphasized. Fear of crime and its reactions help keep the gender hierarchy intact by legitimizing notions based on biological presuppositions (i.e., of differences in physical weakness and strength) and by presenting them as "natural." Some rituals of protection also maintain social relations that are divisive because they are classist, racist, or homophobic.

Many of the rituals of protection infantilize women by presenting them as defenseless and always in need of shelter and protection from others. Several adult and even elderly women often used phrases such as, "I am not allowed to go into the subway," or "My boyfriend does not allow me to take night classes," without questioning the fact that adult women have the right and ability to make their own decisions. Moreover, under the theme that it is "for their own good," women are coerced to impose limits upon their activities.

The everyday negotiations into which women have entered in order to handle their fear of crime happen "within the framework of constraints, both material and ideological" (Green et al. 1991). Studies show that women practice a greater variety and a larger number of protection rituals than do men, demonstrating their feelings of greater vulnerability to violence (Stanko 1990, 14, 15). Paradoxically, several women in this study said that they were accused by their male counterparts of being overly cautious. In fact, several of them said that they had been charged with being "paranoid." One of them, Ruth, a middle-class white woman, said:

Probably I am paranoid, as my husband says. But how do I know if it is my paranoia or it is a reality? Just turn the TV on and open the newspapers and look what you see there! And then, if I am not paranoid and something happens to me or my children, probably he would be the first to say, "See, you were not careful enough. Don't you know better?" *damned either way*

As Ruth expressed, some accusers could easily become the first to blame women if something bad happens to them. Since men are in an entirely different social position, it is difficult for them to fully grasp the complexity of the daily negotiations whereby women must deal with anxieties about their safety. Another of the participants, Alison, a Latina woman, said:

When have you seen that a man has to do everything that we have to do every day to protect ourselves? Watch the way you dress, hold your bag in a certain way, look strong and secure of yourself, sometimes even mean, hide your jewelry, ignore nasty comments.

Alison's narrative deals with an important and neglected issue: many men cannot comprehend the annoyances and irritations that a woman has to endure daily in order to protect herself and feel safer. Rather than "paranoid" or "irrational," fear of crime is a violation of women's rights and should be considered as such. Although most women are aware of and disturbed by the daily constraints that fear of crime imposes upon them, the public is not generally aware that the rights of women are violated as a result of such fears. Many of the participants reported how fear of crime limits their participation in church activities, recycling activities, and volunteer work. It also interferes with their right to participate in leisure activities and to use public space. Women's rights to fulfilling and gratifying jobs and to education are often severely limited by the fear of crime. If fear of crime is seen within the framework of women's rights, it will become part of the national and international agendas of human rights and women's rights agencies. As Jane Roberts Chapman points out, widespread violence against women and its tolerance constitute a problem which has been ignored or has not been recognized as a human rights problem (1990). The fear arising from women's sense of their susceptibility to violence and abuse is also a neglected women's rights issue, one which is aggravated by the lack of an official response to it.

Efforts aimed at providing services to women victims in the aftermath of a crime may decrease their fear. Battered women's shelters, rape intervention centers, hot lines, and similar services have provided some women with the necessary support to leave abusers or to confront rapists. Although such efforts do not necessarily challenge the structures that keep women in a subordinate position, they do provide a respite from abuse (Stanko 1990). Some of these services raise women's consciousness about the roots of the private violence and the dangers they face. They also grant women the opportunity to break their silence about violent acts committed against them by relatives and acquaintances. Such services must recognize the specific needs of women of color as well as immigrant and undocumented women. In the case of Latina women, cultural and language barriers—and often immigration status—prevent them from seeking help at a shelter or from reporting a rape. Therefore, efforts should be directed at encouraging the development of informal community net-

works to offer support in cases of domestic abuse, incest, and acquaintance rape.

The official response to the fear of crime has been to increase the
number of police officers on the streets. Many of the participants in
this study, however, especially young women of color, reported feeling unsafe in the presence of police. In addition, research on fear re-
duction strategies, such as those carried out in Newark, New Jersey,
and in Houston, Texas, suggest that police presence does not reduce
the fear of crime (Pate et al. 1986). Efforts to sensitize the police and
fight stereotypes and prejudices among officers could increase community trust in the work of the police and thus decrease fear of crime.
In their famous article, "Broken Windows: The Police and Neighborhood Safety," criminologists James Q. Wilson and George Kelling
(1982) called for a return to last-century-style community policing, in
which police walk the beat, maintain a presence in the community,
and inspire feelings of public safety. Samuel Walker (1984) has criti-
cized the "broken windows" concept of community policing presented
by Wilson and Kelling, charging that it distorts history by romanticiz-
ing the role of the police. The reality, Walker says, is that old-style police officers were neither liked nor respected. Efforts to understand
the role of the police and other criminal justice agencies in decreasing fear of crime must continue, but attempts aimed at decreasing
fear of crime should not rely only on the work of criminal justice agencies. It is unreasonable and naive to pretend that criminal justice
agencies can control either fear or crime, since both result from dis-
parate power relations. Besides, bureaucratic justice agencies, the
police, the courts, and the prisons are important forces in maintaining
and reinforcing such relations.

The vocabulary of crime and fear of crime needs to be carefully examined. It is profoundly offensive to certain sectors of the population
because it contains openly derogatory terms as well as code words
that—although seemingly inoffensive—continually stigmatize specific behaviors and groups. Crime has, indeed, become code language
for race, class, and gender. The general public should be made aware
of the way in which such vocabulary is derogatory and stigmatizing.
Because of their influence on their audiences, reporters, editors, TV
commentators, and radio commentators must be held especially

responsible for their language. Images of criminals and victims have a profound unconscious and emotional influence on the public, shaping people's fears; influencing and reinforcing everyday discourse about crime, criminals, and victims; and, eventually, shaping criminal justice practices. Discussions about crime must be presented in an accurate manner, without the alarmist outrage or the moral panic provoked by individual crimes. Heinous crimes committed against children, women, and the elderly will always produce and should produce a sense of moral indignation. The public must take a strong stand against crime, especially against heinous and senseless acts of violence and hate, many of them committed against women, minorities, and homosexuals. Problems arise when attempts are made to pass or change legislation or criminal justice practices in response to highly publicized crimes, many of which are rare, no matter how outrageous they are to us, for these decisions influence the lives of millions of people. Legislating by fear and not by serious and emotionally detached attempts to understand true patterns of criminal behavior and devise programs that help decrease crime misleads the public who believe that "something is being done."

Conscientious criminologists should use their access to the media to expose the reality of crime and to educate the public. But, most importantly, the public should demand accurate information and reporting denouncing the politics of backlash (especially directed against young women and men of color and immigrants) and the fear promoted by those who attempt to push their conservative agendas by manipulating public fears and anxieties. Examples of accurate reporting are sparse, but are already taking place. Some of them include recent attempts to educate the public about the chances of a woman's being assaulted or even killed by a stranger, versus the possibilities of being the victim of murder or sexual assault by an acquaintance.

Victimology, as a discipline, has been co-opted by conservatives and advocates of the law-and-order model, who have introduced an individualistic bias that severely limits our ability to explain patterns of victimization (Walklate 1990) and fear. Fear of crime, particularly, has been studied mainly from the perspective of positivistic criminology, which focuses on the physical, social, and economic characteristics of those individuals who are more afraid of crime. Positivistic criminology also disregards the connections between people's anxieties about crime and the broader structures of power.

New models of scholarship to study fear of crime have emerged with the efforts of a handful of U.S. and British criminologists who have begun to develop a feminist victimology and criminology. Feminist studies of fear of crime from scholars such as Elizabeth Stanko (1993, 1991, 1990), Carol Brooks Gardner (1995), Jalna Hanmer and Sheila Saunders (1984), Margaret Gordon and Stephanie Riger (1991), as well as the study presented in this book, are promising. They examine fear of crime and the everyday negotiations that women have to enter into within the framework of dominance and subordination between men and women and gay and straight individuals of different racial backgrounds, and between the rich and the poor. As these studies imply, keeping women afraid is one more way to maintain control of those who are considered vulnerable.

As Anthony Giddens (1984) has argued, barriers between quantitative and qualitative research methodologies should be surmounted. Both have limitations as well as advantages. Whereas quantitative studies measure patterns of victimization and fear, qualitative studies offer in-depth examinations of the images and themes that inform women's fears and seek out the roots of such images as well. Feminist studies have shown that the sole reliance on survey questionnaires and official statistics can be problematic because of their exclusion of important sectors of the population (Walklate 1990). Local victimization surveys, such as the Islington Crime Survey in Great Britain (Crawford et al. 1990), which make every effort to include in their samples an adequate representation of people of color and youth—for whom victimization and fear of crime are a constant menace—are a step in the right direction. These local surveys target specific areas where crime constitutes a serious problem and ask questions about crimes such as child abuse and violation of safety regulations at work, which are not included in the official victimization surveys (Walklate 1990, 28). Ethnographic studies in the form of narratives using focus groups, in-depth interviews, journals, and individual and collective testimonies must be incorporated and given the recognition that they deserve within criminology and victimology. The particular methodologies used in this book—focus groups and in-depth interviews—

encouraged women to express their experiences and to open their lives to each other and to me. These two methodological techniques were instrumental in helping to understand how coercively the fear of crime acts upon women's lives and how this coercion varies according to social circumstance.

The fear of crime unmistakably serves to control and limit women's activities, creating public acquiescence about actions that are "appropriate" or "inappropriate" for women to engage in. Although many of the protective strategies that women use may well reduce their victimization and their fear of crime, they also perpetuate stereotypical notions about women as vulnerable and passive and men as strong, forceful, and aggressive. Moreover, most women and men respond to their fears through individual efforts within the system, maintaining and supporting existing social relations, rather than through efforts—individual and collective—that challenge existing structures of power. In addition to imposing severe limitations upon their activities, fear of crime is an everyday reminder of the subordinate position that women continue to occupy within U.S. society as we close the twentieth century and approach the second millennium.

Despite my mother's advice—exemplified in the title of this book—we know that in fact many bad things happen to "good girls." And, some women refuse to constrain their lives to be good girls in spite of frequent admonitions. Furthermore, it seems that fearless women are considered bad girls because they challenge prevailing power structures.

Appendix A

How We Study Fear of Crime

Many studies of the fear of crime use quantitative data from the NCVS and the General Social Survey (Box et al. 1988; Covington and Taylor 1991; Garofalo 1979; Skogan and Maxfield 1981; Taylor and Covington 1993). Some researchers have collected their own data by surveying individuals in particular cities or neighborhoods (LaGrange and Ferraro 1989; Warr 1984). For this social constructionist study I believed it necessary to listen to women's voices in order to explain some of the patterns that I and others have found in these quantitative studies. Moreover, some authors have suggested that individuals who are more afraid of crime would not answer questions asked by a stranger knocking at their door or calling them on the telephone. Thus, rather than using quantitative methodology, this book relies entirely on women's stories. It uses information from focus groups and in-depth interviews conducted in New York City and surrounding suburban areas, including small towns in northern New Jersey and upstate New York. Between October 1994 and the fall of 1995, I conducted eighteen focus groups with white, Black, and Latina women of different ages: teenagers, adults, and seniors. The women were also from different socioeconomic backgrounds: from a group of homeless African American teenagers in Manhattan to a group of middle-class white women in the suburbs of northern New Jersey. In addition, I conducted thirty in-depth interviews, one on one and face to face, with women from different socioeconomic, racial, and age groups.

The reason for doing individual interviews was to consider also the opinions of some women without the possible influence of ideas and attitudes expressed by the members of the focus groups. The thirty in-depth interviews and eighteen focus groups conducted for this study lasted between one and two hours each, the in-depth interviews tending to be shorter than the focus group sessions. The total number of participants in the study was 140.

These complementary qualitative methodologies are not designed to discover how many women share certain characteristics. They are aimed at gaining access to the way women construct and express their views and images of crimes, criminals, victims, and their interconnections. Unlike survey questionnaires, which are restricted to fixed questions and short answers, the focus group and in-depth interviews encourage the exchange of ideas in a nonrestrictive atmosphere.

Focus groups were originally developed during the early 1940s, when Robert Merton was invited by Paul Lazarsfeld to evaluate the response of some individuals to radio programs at the Office of Radio Research at Columbia University, in New York City (Stewart and Shamdasani 1990). Since then the technique has been utilized in market research, and more recently it has become popular in social research. The advantages of focus groups are various. First, the researcher can interview several persons at once. Second, the focus group produces a large and rich amount of information expressed in the participants' own voices. Third, in my own experience, the group dynamic stimulates the free flow of ideas, bringing to light aspects of the topic that the researcher may not have previously considered. Fourth, although the moderator decides on the questions beforehand and organizes them into a discussion guide, the researcher's views are less strongly imposed on the interviewees than when survey questionnaires are used. In many of the focus groups I led, the participants brought to my attention issues I had not previously considered. The interview guide was flexible enough to enable me to listen to the language of the women, allowing the discussion to move in a direction that was meaningful to them, while at the same time preserving the structure needed for comparisons between groups.

Focus groups are an especially sensitive methodology for women in general, and for Latina immigrant women in particular, some of whom have told me they felt comfortable in this nonthreatening group setting. As one of the participants explained, "When I am alone with an interviewer, I feel intimidated, scared. And if they call me over the telephone, I never answer their questions. How do I know what they really want or who they are?" The method also allowed me to include undocumented women, who, because they were interviewed not individually but in the company of other undocumented and documented women, were more open to participating in the discussion. The focus group sessions were conducted in English or in Spanish, according to the preference of the group.

Focus groups have been used both to explore new topics and to confirm or substantiate the results of past studies. In the case of fear of crime, many previous studies have shed some light on who is more fearful in their neighborhoods, or on some of the factors associated with fear of crime, such as the presence of physical incivilities—trash, graffiti, broken windows, abandoned buildings (Taylor et al. 1984; Taylor and Covington 1993). This information helps to explain the general patterns of fear. Because of their quantitative nature, however, these studies do not provide us with in-depth information about how these fears affect women in different social domains and what the possible roots of these fears are. They also fail to capture the wealth of information contained in the many images and symbols associated with women's fear of crime, their impact on women's everyday lives, and the various rituals women use to deal with their fears and anxieties.

This study used focus groups and in-depth interviews to achieve a deeper understanding of women and their concerns about crime. The purpose of the study is not to disclose who is more afraid of crime, what variables shape people's fear, or what socioeconomic or neighborhood characteristics trigger individuals' feelings regarding crime. Rather, it is to hear women explain how they imagine crime and how their everyday rituals are affected by the images associated with it.

Focus groups and in-depth interviews are a form of collective and individual testimony. They are excellent tools for recovering and using the knowledge acquired from women's daily experience. These testimonies enable women to break the wall of silence enclosing their ideas and emotions. In reality, women have used testimonies for generations in the form of exchanges with mothers, sisters, neighbors, friends. Caricatured as "gossip" in a male-centered culture, such exchanges have traditionally been a major way in which women have dealt with the social isolation imposed upon them. Furthermore, such testimonies, individual or collective, are an excellent vehicle for capturing the socioeconomic, political, and human voices of women (Randall 1980).

The advantage of the focus group as a form of collective testimony is that it enables women to exchange and validate their shared experiences with other women of similar socioeconomic and ethnic backgrounds (Jarrett 1993). The group interaction emphasizes empathy and commonality of experiences and fosters greater self-disclosure as well as self-validation. Communication among women can be an awakening experience and an important element in the process of consciousness-raising. Such communication asserts women's right to confirm and verify their own experience, which in many instances has been defined by men or presented from a man's viewpoint. The discovery that other women experience similar problems and have similar ideas is an important tool in helping women face their problems and validate their opinions.

As with any other research technique, focus groups are not without disadvantages. The conversation deviates very easily from the topic. The moderator must skillfully obtain information that may be relevant without getting completely off track, a difficult task but also an educational one. Also, in some instances one participant, emerging as a natural leader of the group, may monopolize the conversation and lead the group in one direction. My teaching experience, however, prepared me to draw participants into the conversation and encourage dissent by explaining to the group at the outset that it was appropriate.

Major difficulties can arise in organizing focus groups and contacting participants. Being connected to community leaders and organizations proved crucial. They, together with my students, were the most important means of recruitment. Generally I contacted a person who in turn organized the group under my guidance.

It was especially important for this study that each focus group be homogenous in race, class, and age, since I believed that participants would feel more free to discuss their images of crime, criminals, and victims with other women like themselves. Explaining this need to group organizers was a sensitive issue requiring careful explanation. On several occasions meetings had to be canceled at the last minute because participants could not come. Flexibility was a major virtue during those times.

From the total sample of 140 participants in the homogenous focus groups and in-depth interviews, 43 were white, 38 Black and 59 Latina (Black, white, or racially mixed women of Latin origin). The age distribution was as follows: 47 teenagers (ages 13 to 19), 62 adults (ages 20 to 59), and 31 seniors (60 and older). The sample intentionally overrepresented minority and teenage women. Since the majority of studies on fear of crime underrepresent these groups and very few even consider teenage and Latina women, it was necessary to give special attention to their voices. In the case of participants under eighteen years of age, a consent letter was sent to their parents a few days before the interview, explaining the project and requesting parental authorization for their daughter's participation.

The groups involved between five and twelve participants. They sat together around a dinner table or in the living room of a participant's home, or in a classroom, and discussed the impact of fear of crime upon their lives. I acted as a moderator in all focus groups except one, which was led by one of my students. My role was to ask some questions and to be sure that the participants felt comfortable and open in talking about the theme. With the permission of the participants, the discussions were taped and later transcribed.

The interviewees were all volunteers. Some were recruited through referrals from other participants, some were students, and some had attended one of my presentations or had heard through third parties about my research topic and wanted to be interviewed. The sample, therefore, is one of availability and convenience, recruited through a revised process of snow-balling (Morse 1992). Since the sample is neither random nor representative of the U.S. population, I avoid generalizations throughout the text (McCracken 1988). The intent of this study is not generalizability but of accessibility to women and their views and images regarding fear of crime.

The focus groups took me to a wide variety of places: from the basement of an alternative school in a Latino neighborhood in Manhattan to the dinner table of a middle-class white woman in the suburbs of New Jersey; from the living room of an elderly woman who served tea and exquisite pastries to the floor of a teenager's house where pizza and soft drinks were set out. The in-depth interviews were also carried out in a variety of locations: classrooms, participant's living rooms, and my office at Hunter College were common places.

I met the women when and where it was most convenient for them. As much as possible, I adapted my schedule to meet their needs. I considered myself privileged to be admitted into their lives for a couple of hours and to be granted a glimpse at their social reality.

The chapters of this book present the findings of these discussion groups and in-depth interviews. Although I often refer to the participants by name, I have changed all names to protect their identities, and, moreover, I have given only the general names and locations of their towns and neighborhoods. Naming towns or neighborhoods could have jeopardized participants' confidentiality, since some mentioned incidents that occurred in institutions in their communities, such as schools. Furthermore, some contact people and participants commented that their neighborhoods were often portrayed by the media as "dangerous"; my respect for their feelings and my admiration for their community work obliged me to protect the identity of those locations.

I was loyal to women's expressions as much as possible. In other words, I tried not to edit their words. Only in a very few cases, when it would have been difficult for a reader to understand what they were saying, did I take some liberties. I translated interviews conducted in Spanish, being careful to use the English words that, in my judgment as a bilingual and bicultural person, best corresponded to their expressions. When I thought that only a Spanish word could communicate the women's sentiments and illustrate the vitality of an expression, I wrote the word in italics and followed it with the English translation.

Although I occasionally use numbers to explain how many women express similar ideas, I am not interested in the numbers in and of themselves. The primary purpose of this study is to understand women's fears and their representations of crime, criminals, and victims. I therefore use expressions such as *frequently, in general,* or *most women* to reflect the various responses that emerged from the majority of women's voices.

Throughout the book I use the terms *Black* and *African American,* as well as *Latina* and *Hispanic,* interchangeably. Because the Bureau of Justice Statistics and the U.S. Bureau of Census use the terms *Black* and *Hispanic* in their data, I usually follow their designation when I am dealing with such data. The women often used these terms as synonyms; in attempting to be loyal to their voices, I follow their usage.

This is not a book about women as victims of their fears. Some of the women said they were not afraid of crime. Others indicated that although they were not afraid, they did take precautions—a seemingly contradictory response that I did not challenge because I believe that our lives are filled with such inconsistencies and I did not see it as my role to point out these discrepancies.

Although some may find the women's strategies for dealing with their fears appealing, others may not be inspired by their coping mechanisms. The information provided by the participants will nevertheless help us understand the sociostructural conditions that underlie fear of crime and the everyday rituals women use to deal with it, and thus provide insights about the roots of such fears and how to fight against the negative consequences.

References

Adler, Freda. 1975. *Sisters in Crime: The Rise of the New Female Criminal.* New York: McGraw-Hill.

Adler, Jerry. 1994. "Kids Growing Up Scared." *Newsweek,* 10 January, 43–49.

Advertising Age. 1994. "Numbers for the 90s. Safer Shopping." 29 August, 3.

Allende, Isabel. 1993. *The House of the Spirits.* New York: Bantam.

American Correctional Association. 1992. *Juvenile and Adult Correctional Departments, Institutions, Agencies, and Paroling Authorities.* Laurel, Md.: American Correctional Association.

Amin, Menachem. 1971. *Patterns of Forcible Rape.* Chicago: University of Chicago Press.

Andersen, Margaret. 1993. *Thinking about Women: Sociological Perspectives on Sex and Gender.* New York: Macmillan.

Balkin, Steven. 1979. "Victimization Rates, Safety, and Fear of Crime." *Social Problems* 26: 343–58.

Balkin, Steven, and P. Houlden. 1983. "Reducing Fear of Crime through Occupational Presence." *Criminal Justice and Behavior* 10: 13–33.

Barak, Gregg. 1994a. "Between the Waves: Mass-Mediated Themes of Crime and Justice." *Social Justice* 21: 133–47.

———. 1994b. "Mediated Crime and the ACJS." *ACJS Today* (November/December): 3.

Baumer, Terry. 1985. "Testing a General Model of Fear of Crime." *Journal of Research in Crime and Delinquency* 22: 239–55.

Becker, Howard. 1964. *The Other Side: Perspectives on Deviance.* New York: The Free Press.

Bell, Alan P., and Martin S. Weinberg. 1978. *Homosexualities: A Study of Diversity among Men and Women.* New York: Simon and Schuster.

Benedict, Helen. 1992. *Virgin or Vamp: How the Press Covers Sex Crimes.* New York: Oxford University Press.

Ben-Yehuda, Nachman. 1986. "The Sociology of Moral Panics: Toward a New Synthesis." *The Sociological Quarterly* 24: 495–513.

Berger, Peter L., and Thomas Luckmann. 1967. *The Social Construction of Reality*. New York: Anchor Books.

Berke, Richard. 1994a. "Crime Is Becoming Nations' Top Fear." *New York Times*. 23 January, A-21.

———. 1994b. "Survey Finds Voters in the U.S. Rootless and Self-Absorbed." *New York Times*, 21 September, A-21.

Bland, Lucy. 1992. "The Case of the Yorkshire Ripper: Mad, Bad, Beast or Male." In Jill Radford and Diana E. H. Russell, eds., *Femicide: The Politics of Woman Killing*. 233–52. New York: Twayne.

Bohn, Ted S. 1983–84. "Homophobic Violence: Implications for Social Work Practice." *Journal of Social Work and Human Sexuality* 2: 91–112.

Box, Steven, Chris Hale, and Glenn Andrews. 1988. "Explaining Fear of Crime." *British Journal of Criminology* 28: 340–56.

Braungart, Margaret, Richard Braungart, and William Hoyer. 1980. "Age, Sex, and Social Factors in Fear of Crime." *Sociological Focus* 13: 55–66.

Brownmiller, Susan. 1975. *Against Our Will: Men, Women, and Rape*. New York: Fawcett Columbine.

Bureau of Justice Statistics. 1996. *Criminal Victimization in the United States, 1994*. Washington, D.C.: U.S. Department of Justice.

———. 1995a. *Sourcebook of Criminal Justice Statistics, 1994*. Washington, D.C.: U.S. Department of Justice.

———. 1995b. *Guns Used in Crime*. Washington, D.C.: U.S. Department of Justice.

———. 1995c. *Violence against Women: Estimates from the Redesigned Survey*. Washington, D.C.: U.S. Department of Justice.

———. 1994a. *Violence between Intimates*. Washington, D.C.: U.S. Department of Justice.

———. 1994b. *Source Book of Criminal Justice Statistics, 1993*. Washington, D.C.: U.S. Department of Justice.

———. 1992. *Survey of State Prison Inmates, 1991*. Washington, D.C.: U.S. Department of Justice.

———. 1991. *Prisoners in 1990*. Washington, D.C.: U.S. Department of Justice.

Butterfield, Fox. 1995. "More Blacks in Their 20's Have Trouble with the Law." *New York Times*, 5 October, A-18.

Cain, Maureen. 1989. "Feminists Transgress Criminology." In Maureen Cain, ed., *Growing Up Good: Policing the Behavior of Girls in Europe*. Newbury Park, Calif.: Sage Publications.

Carlen, Pat. 1994. "Gender, Class, Racism, and Criminal Justice: Against Global and Gender-Centric Theories, for Poststructuralist Perspectives."

In George S. Bridges and Martha Myers, eds., *Inequality, Crime, and Social Control*, 134–44. Boulder, Colo.: Westview Press.

Carr, C. 1995. "The Politics of Sin." *The Village Voice,* 16 May, 26–30.

Chamberlain, Pam. 1985. "Homophobia in the Schools, or What We Don't Know Will Hurt Us." *Radical Teacher* 29: 3–6.

Chambliss, William J., and Robert B. Seidman. 1971. *The Social Reality of Crime.* Reading, Mass.: Addison Wesley.

Chancer, Lynn S. 1992. *Sadomasochism in Everyday Life: The Dynamics of Power and Powerlessness.* New Brunswick, N.J.: Rutgers University Press.

Chapman, Jane Roberts. 1990. "Women, Violence and Human Rights," *Social Justice* 17: 54–70.

Chesney-Lind, Meda. 1995. "Rethinking Women's Imprisonment: A Critical Examination of Trends in Female Incarceration." In Barbara Raffel Price and Natalie Sokoloff, eds., *The Criminal Justice System and Women,* 105–17. New York: McGraw-Hill.

Chira, Susan. 1994. "Solomon's Rules for the 90's." *New York Times,* 25 September, sec. 4, 1, 3.

Christie, Nils. 1986. "The Ideal Victim." In Ezzat A. Fattah, ed., *From Crime Policy to Victim Policy,* 17–30. New York: St. Martin's Press.

Clarke, Ronald. 1983. "Situational Crime Prevention: Its Theoretical Basis and Practical Scope." In Michael Tonry and Norval Morris, eds., *Annual Review of Criminal Justice Research,* 225–56. Chicago: University of Chicago Press.

Clemente, Frank, and Michael B. Kleiman. 1977. "Fear of Crime in the United States: A Multivariate Analysis." *Social Forces* 56: 518–31.

Clymer, Adam. 1995. "Cocaine Terms Unchanged." Congressional Roundup. *New York Times,* 13 September, A-18.

Cohen, Lawrence, and Marcus Felson. 1979. "Social Change and Crime Rate Trends: A Routine Activities Approach." *American Sociological Review* 44: 588–608.

Cohen, Lawrence E., James R. Kluegel, and Kenneth C. Land. 1981. "Social Inequality and Predatory Criminal Victimization: An Exposition and Test of a Formal Theory." *American Sociological Review* 48: 505–24.

Comstock, Gary D. 1991. *Violence against Lesbians and Gay Men.* New York: Columbia University Press.

Cose, Ellis. 1990. "Turning Victims into Saints." *Time,* 22 January, 19.

Covington, Jeanette, and Ralph Taylor. 1991. "Fear of Crime in Urban Residential Neighborhoods: Implications of Between—and Within—Neighborhood Sources for Current Models." *Sociological Quarterly* 32: 231–49.

Crawford, A., T. Jones, T. Woodhouse, and J. Young. 1990. Second Islington Crime Survey. London: Middlesex Polytechnic.

Cunningham, William, John Strauchs, and Clifford Van Meter. 1991. "Private Security Patterns and Trends." *NIJ Research in Brief.* Washington, D.C.: U.S. Department of Justice.

Currie, Elliott. 1985. *Confronting Crime.* New York: Pantheon.

———. 1968. "Crimes without Criminals: Witchcraft and Its Control in Renaissance Europe." *Law and Society Review* 3: 7–32.

de Certeau, Michel. 1984. *The Practice of Everyday Life.* Berkeley: University of California Press.

DuBow, Frederick, Edward McCabe, and Gail Kaplan. 1979. *Reactions to Crime: A Critical Review of the Literature.* Washington, D.C.: National Institute of Law Enforcement and Criminal Justice.

Durkheim, Emile. 1982. *The Rules of the Sociological Method and Selected Texts on Sociology and Its Method.* New York: The Free Press.

Dworkin, Andrea. 1974. *Woman Hating.* New York: Dutton.

Dwyer, Jim. 1994. "A Mad Affair of Drugs, Jails," *New York Newsday,* 14 September, A-2.

Ehrenreich, Barbara, and Deidre English. 1978. *For Her Own Good: 150 Years of the Experts' Advice to Women.* New York: Doubleday.

Elshtain, Jean Bethke. 1995. *Democracy on Trial.* New York: Basic Books.

Erikson, Kai. 1966. *Wayward Puritans: A Study in the Sociology of Deviance.* New York: Wiley.

Estrich, Susan. 1994. "The Last Victim." *New York Times Magazine,* 18 December, 54, 55.

Faith, Karlene. 1993. *Unruly Women. The Politics of Confinement and Resistance.* Vancouver: Press Gang Publishers.

Faludi, Susan. 1991. *Backlash: The Undeclared War against American Women.* New York: Crown.

Federal Bureau of Investigation. 1993. *Crime in the United States 1992.* Washington, D. C.: U.S. Government Printing Office.

Ferraro, Kenneth F., and Randy LaGrange. 1987. "The Measurement of Fear of Crime," *Sociological Inquiry* 57: 70–101.

Firestone, Shulamith. 1971. *The Dialectic of Sex.* London: Paladin.

Fox, James Alan, and Jack Levin. 1994. *Overkill: Mass Murder and Serial Killing Exposed.* New York: Plenum.

Friedman, Josh. 1993. "Emigres Living in Fear." *New York Newsday,* 22 December, 4, 99.

Gardner, Carol Brooks. 1995. *Passing By: Gender and Public Harassment.* Berkeley: University of California Press.

Garofalo, James. 1979. "Victimization and Fear of Crime." *Journal of Research in Crime and Delinquency* 16: 80–97.

———. 1977. *Public Opinion About Crime: The Attitudes of Victims and Non-victims in Selected Cities.* U.S. Department of Justice, National

Criminal Justice Information and Statistics Service. Washington, D.C.: U.S. Government Printing Office.

Garofalo, Raffaelo. 1914. *Criminology*. Boston: Little, Brown.

Gelles, Richard, and Murray Strauss. 1979. "Violence in the American Family," *Journal of Social Issues* 35: 15–39.

Giddens, Anthony. 1984. *The Constitution of Society*. Cambridge, U.K.: Polity Press.

Goode, Erich, and Nachman Ben-Yehuda. 1994. *Moral Panics: The Social Construction of Deviance*. Oxford, U.K.: Blackwell.

Gordon, Margaret T., and Stephanie Riger. 1991. *The Female Fear: The Social Cost of Rape*. Chicago: University of Illinois Press.

Gove, Walter. 1985. "The Effects of Age and Gender on Deviant Behavior: A Biopsychological Perspective." In Alice S. Rossi, ed., *Gender and the Life Course*, 115–43. Hawthorne, N.Y.: Aldine.

Green, Eileen, Sandra Hebron, and Diana Woodward. 1991. "Women, Leisure, and Social Control." In Jalna Hanmer and Mary Maynard, eds., *Women, Violence and Social Control*, 75–92. Atlantic Highlands, N.J.: Humanities Press International.

Greenberg, David. 1977. "The Dynamics of Oscillatory Punishment Processes." *Journal of Criminal Law and Criminology* 68: 643–51.

Greenfeld, Lawrence, and James Stephan. 1993. *Capital Punishment 1992*. Washington, D.C.: Bureau of Justice Statistics.

Griffin, Susan. 1971. "Rape: The All-American Crime." *Ramparts* 10 (September): 35.

"Guns Gaining on Cars as a Leading U.S. Killer." *The New York Times*, 26 Jan 1994, A-12.

Hall, Stuart, Chas Critcher, Tony Jefferson, John Clarke, and Brian Roberts. 1978. *Policing the Crisis: Mugging, the State and Law and Order*. New York: Holmes and Meier.

Hanmer, Jalna, and Sheila Saunders. 1984. *Well-founded Fear: A Community Study of Violence Against Women*. London: Hutchinson.

Heidensohn, Frances. 1985. *Women and Crime: The Life of the Female Offender*. New York: New York University Press.

Hester, Marianne. 1992. "The Witch-craze in Sixteenth and Seventeenth Century England as Social Control of Women." In Jill Radford and Diana E. H. Russell, eds., *Femicide: The Politics of Woman Killing*, 27–39. New York: Twayne.

Hindelang, Michael, Michael R. Gottfredson, and James Garofalo. 1978. *Victims of Personal Crime: An Empirical Foundation of a Theory of Personal Victimization*. Cambridge, Mass.: Ballinger.

Holmes, Steven A. 1996. "Income Disparity Between Poorest and Richest Rises." *New York Times*, 20 June, A-1, A-25.

————. 1994. "Ranks of Inmates Reach One Million in a 2-Decade Rise." *New York Times,* 28 October, A-1, A-25.

Horowitz, Joy. 1994. "Arms and the Woman." *Harper's Bazaar,* February, 166–9.

"In 1994, Vote for Woman Does not Play so Well." *The New York Times,* 3 October 1994, A-1, B-10.

Jankovic, Ivan. 1977. "Labor Market and Imprisonment." *Crime and Social Justice* 8: 17–31.

Jarrett, Robin L. 1993. "Focus Group Interviews with Low-Income Minority Populations: A Research Experience." In David L. Morgan, ed., *Successful Focus Groups. Advancing the State of the Art,* 184–201. Newbury Park, Calif.: Sage.

Jenkins, Philip. 1992. *Intimate Enemies: Moral Panics in Contemporary Britain.* New York: Aldine de Gruyter.

Johns, Christina. 1992. *Power, Ideology, and the War on Drugs. Nothing Succeeds Like Failure.* New York: Praeger.

"Jury Selection Begins in the Polly Klaas Case," *The New York Times,* 12 July 1995 A-12.

Kelly, Liz. 1991. "The Continuum of Sexual Violence." In Jalna Hanmer and Mary Maynard, eds., *Women, Violence, and Social Control,* 46–60. Atlantic Highlands, N.J.: Humanity Press International.

Kinkead, Gwen. 1994. "Spock, Brazelton, and Now . . . Penelope Leach." *New York Times Magazine,* 10 April, 32–5.

Klein, Doris. 1995. "The Etiology of Female Crime: A Review of the Literature." In Barbara Raffel Price and Natalie J. Sokoloff, eds., *The Criminal Justice System and Women: Offenders, Victims, and Workers,* 30–53. New York: McGraw-Hill.

Kunkle, Frederick. 1995. "Mugger Kills Honor Student, 20." *The Record,* 15 July, A-1, A-7.

LaGrange, Randy L., and Kenneth Ferraro. 1989. "Assessing Age and Gender Differences in Perceived Risk and Fear of Crime." *Criminology* 27: 697–718.

Lewin, Tamar. 1994. "What Penalty for a Killing in Passion?" *New York Times,* 21 October, A-18.

Liazos, Alexander. 1982. *People First: An Introduction to Social Problems.* Boston: Allyn and Bacon.

Liska, Allen, and Barbara D. Warner. 1991. "Functions of Crime: A Paradoxical Process." *American Journal of Sociology* 96: 1441–63.

Liska, Allen, Joseph Lawrence, and Andrew Sanchirico. 1991. "Fear of Crime as a Social Fact." *Social Forces* 60: 760–70.

Llorente, Elizabeth. 1995. "Young Toughs Terrorize Illegal Aliens." *The Record,* 17 February, A-1, A-12.

MacKinnon, Catharine. 1993. "Feminism, Marxism, Method, and the State: Toward a Feminist Jurisprudence." In Pauline B. Bart and Eileen Geil Moran. *Violence Against Women, The Bloody Footprints*, 201–27. Newbury Park, Calif.: Sage.

———. 1987. *Feminism Unmodified*. Cambridge, Mass.: Harvard University Press.

Madriz, Esther. 1992. *Fear of Crime and Victimization of Women: A Real Paradox?* Ph.D. diss., Vanderbilt University.

Males, Mike. 1994. "Unwed Mothers: The Wrong Target." *New York Times*, 29 July, A-15.

Manis, Jerome. 1974. *Analyzing Social Problems*. New York: Praeger, 25.

Manis, Jerome. 1974. "The Concept of Social Problems: Vox Populis and Sociological Analysis." *Social Problems* 21: 301–15.

Mann, Coramae Richey. 1995. "Women of Color and the Criminal Justice System." In Barbara Raffel Price and Natalie Sokoloff, eds., *The Criminal Justice System and Women*, 118–35. New York: McGraw-Hill.

———. 1993. *Unequal Justice. A Question of Color.* Bloomington: Indiana University Press.

Mauer, Mark. 1991. *Americans Behind Bars: A Comparison of International Rates of Incarceration*. Washington, D.C.: The Sentencing Project.

Maxfield, Michael. 1984. "The Limits of Vulnerability in Explaining Fear of Crime: A Comparative Neighborhood Analysis." *Journal of Research in Crime and Delinquency* 21: 233–50.

McCracken, Grant. 1988. *The Long Interview*. Newbury Park, Calif.: Sage.

McLarin, Kimberly J. 1994. "Fear Prompts Self-Defense as Crime Comes to College." *New York Times*, 2 September, A-1, B-11.

McLean, Susana. 1995. "The Victim Gets the Blame in Central Park." *New York Times*, 28 September, A-27.

Mendelsohn, Beniamin. 1974. "The Origins of the Doctrine of Victimology." In Israel Drapkin and Emilio Viano, eds., *Victimology*, 3–11. Lexington, Mass.: Lexington Books.

Merton, Robert K., and Robert Nisbet, eds., 1976. *Contemporary Social Problems*. New York: Harcourt Brace Jovanovich.

Messerschmidt, James W. 1986. *Capitalism, Patriarchy, and Crime: Towards a Socialist Feminist Criminology*. Totowa, N.J.: Rowman and Littlefield.

Miller, Brian, and Laud Humphreys. 1980. "Lifestyles and Violence. Homosexual Victims of Assault and Murder." *Qualitative Sociology* 3: 169–85.

Mitchell, Juliet. 1971. *Woman's State*. New York: Pantheon.

Morrison, Toni. 1994. *Beloved*. New York: Knopf.

Morse, Janice M. 1992. "Strategies for Sampling." In Janice M. Morse, ed., *Qualitative Nursing Research*. Newbury Park, Calif.: Sage, 125–45.

Mullings, Leith. 1994. "Images, Ideology, and Women of Color." In Maxine Bacca Zinn and Bonnie Thornton Dill, eds., *Women of Color in U.S. Society,* 265–289. Philadelphia: Temple University Press.

Nagourney, Adam. "Dole Carries Crime Theme to a Tent Jail." *New York Times,* 18 September, A-13.

Nelson, Lars-Erik. 1995. "Prof. Newt Steers Partisan Course." *New York Newsday,* 18 September, A-13.

Nossiter, Adam. 1994. "Making Hard Time Harder, States Cut Jail TV and Sports." *New York Times,* 17 September, 1, 11.

Ortega, Suzanne T., and Jessie L. Myles. 1987. "Race and Gender Effects on Fear of Crime: An Interactive Model with Age." *Criminology* 25: 133–52.

Pate, Tony, Mary A. Wycoff, Wesley Skogan, and Lawrence W. Sherman. 1986. *Reducing Fear of Crime in Houston and Newark.* Washington, D.C.: Police Foundation.

Pellicani, Luciano. 1981. *Gramsci: An Alternative Communism?* Stanford, Calif.: Hoover Institution Press.

Pérez, Miguel. 1995. "Victimized a 2nd Time." *The Record,* 17 February, C-1.

Piven, Francis, and Richard A. Cloward. 1993. *Regulating the Poor: The Functions of Public Welfare.* New York: Vintage Books.

Platt, Anthony. 1994a. "The Politics of Law and Order." *Social Justice* 21 (3): 3–10.

———. 1994b. "Rethinking and Unthinking Social Control." In George S. Bridges and Martha Myers, eds., *Inequality, Crime, and Social Control,* 72–9. Boulder, Colo.: Westview Press.

Purdum, Todd S. 1996. "Clinton Co-opts Crime Issue, Stressing Victims' Rights." *New York Times,* 27 October, A-14.

Quindlen, Anna. 1994. "Playing Perfect Pattycake. The Mythical Mother." *New York Times,* 13 April, A-21.

Quinney, Richard. 1974. *Critique of the Legal Order.* Boston: Little, Brown.

Radford, Jill. 1991. "Policing Male Violence, Policing Women." In Jalna Hanmer and Mary Maynard, eds., *Women, Violence, and Social Control,* 30–45. Atlantic Highlands, N.J.: Humanities Press International.

Radford, Jill, and Diana E. H. Russell, eds. 1992. *Femicide: The Politics of Woman Killing.* New York: Twayne.

Randall, Margaret. 1980. *Todas Estamos Despiertas.* Ciudad de Mexico, Mexico: Editorial Siglo XXI.

Reiman, Jeffrey. 1995. *The Rich Get Richer and the Poor Get Prison.* Boston, Mass.: Allyn and Bacon.

Riger, Stephanie, and Margaret T. Gordon. 1991. "The Fear of Rape. A Study in Social Control." *Journal of Social Issues* 37: 71–92.

Riger, Stephanie, Margaret T. Gordon, and R. LeBailly. 1978. "Women's Fear of Crime: From Blaming to Restricting the Victim." *Victimology* 3: 274–83.

Rosen, Lawrence, and Kathleen Nelson. 1982. "Broken Homes." In Leonard Savitz and Norman Johnston, eds., *Contemporary Criminology*, 126–35. New York: Wiley.

Roth, Jeffrey A. 1994. "Understanding and Preventing Violence," *National Institute of Justice: Research in Brief.* Washington, D.C.: U.S. Department of Justice.

Rusche, Georg, and Otto Kirchheimer. 1968. *Labor Market and Penal Sanctions: Punishment and Social Structure.* New York: Russell and Russell.

Russell, Diana E. H., ed., 1993. *Making Violence Sexy.* New York: Teachers College Press, Columbia University.

Sagarin, Edward. 1975. *Deviants and Deviancy.* New York: Praeger.

Schwendinger, Herman, and Julia Schwendinger. 1991. "Feminism, Criminology, and Complex Variations." In Brian McLean and Dragan Milovanovic, eds., *New Directions in Critical Criminology: Left Realism, Feminism, Postmodernism, and Peacemaking*, 39–44. Vancouver, Canada: The Collective Press.

Sherman, Rorie. 1995/96. "Crime's Toll on the U.S.: Fear, Despair, and Guns." In John J. Sullivan and Joseph L. Victor, eds., *Annual Editions: Criminal Justice 95/96*, 57. Guilford, Conn.: Dushkin/Brown and Benchmark.

Sidel, Ruth. 1992. *Women and Children Last. The Plight of Poor Women in Affluent America.* New York: Penguin.

Skogan, Wesley. 1987. "The Impact of Victimization on Fear," *Crime and Delinquency* 33: 135–54.

———. 1986. "The Fear of Crime and Its Behavioral Implications." In Ezzat A. Fattah, ed., *From Crime Policy to Victim Policy: Reorienting the Justice System*, 167–188. New York: St. Martin's Press.

Skogan, Wesley, and Michael G. Maxfield. 1981. *Coping with Fear.* Beverly Hills, Calif.: Sage.

Slater, A. S., and S. Feinman. 1985. "Gender and the Phonology of North American First Names." *Sex Roles* 13: 429–40.

Smart, Carol. 1995. *Law, Crime and Sexuality: Essays in Feminism.* London: Sage.

———. 1976. *Women, Crime, and Criminology.* London: Routledge and Kegan Paul.

Smart, Carol, and B. Smart. 1978. *Women, Sexuality, and Social Control.* London: Routledge.

Sparks, Richard. 1992. "Reason and Unreason in 'Left Realism': Some Problems in the Constitution of the Fear of Crime." In Roger Matthews and Jock Young, eds., 119–135. *Issues in Realist Criminology.* London: Sage.

———. 1982. *Research on Victims of Crime: Accomplishments, Issues, and New Directions.* Rockville, Md.: U.S. Department of Health and Human Services, Washington, D.C.

Spindler, Amy M. 1995. "Luxurious Armor by Karan, Klein, Mizrahi." *New York Times*, 8 April, 31.

Spitzer, Steven. 1975. "Toward a Marxian Theory of Deviance." *Social Problems* 22: 638–51.

Stafford, Mark C., and Omer R. Galle. 1984. "Victimization Rates, Exposure to Risk and Fear of Crime." *Criminology* 22: 173–85.

Stanko, Elizabeth. 1993. "Ordinary Fear: Women, Violence, and Personal Safety." In Pauline Bart and Eileen Geil Moran, eds., *Violence Against Women, the Bloody Footprints*, 155–64. Newbury Park, Calif.: Sage.

———. 1991. "Typical Violence, Normal Precaution: Men, Women and Interpersonal Violence in England, Wales, Scotland and the USA." In Jalna Hanmer and Mary Maynard, eds., *Women, Violence, and Social Control*, 122–34. Atlantic Highlands, N.J.: Humanities Press International.

———. 1990. *Everyday Violence: How Women and Men Experience Sexual and Physical Danger.* London: Pandora.

Stewart, Barbara. 1995. "Rebels Against the Rude," *New York Times*, 26 February, sec. 13, 1, 10.

Stewart, David W., and Prem N. Shamdasani. 1990. *Focus Groups: Theory and Practice.* Newbury Park, Calif.: Sage.

Surette, Ray. 1994. "Predator Criminals as Media Icons." In Gregg Barak, ed., *Media, Process, and the Social Construction of Crime: Studies in Newsmaking Criminology*, 131–58. New York: Garland.

———. 1992. *Media, Crime and Criminal Justice: Images and Realities.* Pacific Grove, Calif.: Brooks/Cole.

Szasz, Thomas. 1970. *The Manufacture of Madness.* New York: Dell.

Taylor, Ralph, and Jeanette Covington. 1993. "Community Structural Change and Fear of Crime." *Social Problems* 40: 374–97.

Taylor, Ralph, and Margaret Hale. 1986. "Testing Alternative Models of Fear of Crime." *Journal of Criminal Law and Criminology* 77: 151–89.

Taylor, Ralph, Sally A. Shumaker, and Stephen D. Gottfredson. 1984. "Neighborhood Level Links between Physical Features and Local Sentiments: Deterioration, Fear of Crime, and Confidence." *Journal of Architectural and Planning Research* 2: 261–27.

Todd, Andrea. 1994. "Running Late." *New York Times Magazine*, 6 November, 30.

Toner, Robin. 1994. "Image of Capitol Maligned by Outsiders and Insiders." *New York Times*, 16 October, 1, 24.

Tonry, Michael. 1995. *Malign Neglect: Race, Crime and Punishment in America.* New York: Oxford University Press.

Treaster, Joseph B. 1994. "A Slain Woman's Trail of Pain: Many Contradictions, but Trouble Was Her Constant." *New York Times*, 2 October, 34, 37.

U. S. Bureau of Census. 1990. *Statistical Abstract of the United States.* Washington, D.C.: U.S. Government Printing Office.

U. S. Department of Commerce. 1994. *Bureau of Census, Census Data 1992.* Washington, D.C.: U.S. Government Printing Office.

Vold, George B. 1958. *Theoretical Criminology.* New York: Oxford University Press.

Vold, George B., and Thomas J. Bernard. 1986. *Theoretical Criminology.* New York: Oxford University Press, 270–77.

Von Hentig, Hans. 1948. *The Criminal and His Victim.* New Haven, Conn.: Yale University Press.

Walker, Alice. 1982. *The Color Purple.* New York: Pocket.

Walker, Samuel. 1984. "Broken Windows and Fractured History: The Use and Misuse of History in Recent Police Patrol Analysis." *Justice Quarterly* 1: 75–90.

Walklate, Sandra. 1990. "Researching Victims of Crime: Critical Victimology." *Social Justice* 17: 25–42.

Warr, Mark. 1992. "Altruistic Fear of Victimization." *Social Science Quarterly* 73: 723–36.

———. 1990. "Dangerous Situations: Social Context and Fear of Victimization," *Social Forces* 68: 891–907.

———. 1984. "Fear of Victimization: Why are Women and the Elderly More Afraid?" *Social Science Quarterly* 65: 681–702.

Warr, Mark, and Mark Stafford. 1983. "Fear of Crime: A Look at the Proximate Causes." *Social Forces* 61: 1033–43.

Webster's New American Dictionary. 1995. New York: Smithmark.

West, Cornell. 1993. *Race Matters.* New York: Vintage.

Whitaker, Catherine. 1986. *Crime Prevention Measures.* Washington, D.C.: Bureau of Justice Statistics.

Wilson, James Q., and George Kelling. 1982. "Broken Windows: The Police and Neighborhood Safety." *Atlantic Monthly,* March, 29–38.

"Witness Says Suspect Howled Like Werewolf." *The Record,* 22 April 1994, A-13.

Wolfgang, Marvin. 1958. *Patterns of Criminal Homicide.* Philadelphia: University of Pennsylvania.

Young, Alison. 1996. *Imagining Crime: Textual Outlaws and Criminal Conversations.* London: Sage.

Index

Esther Madriz

Esther Madriz is Assistant Professor of Sociology at the University of San Francisco. She is on the editorial boards of *Social Justice* and *Peace Review,* and has published articles on fear of crime and related topics in academic journals.

Compositor: Publication Services
Text: 11/13.5 Caledonia
Display: Caledonia
Printer: Haddon Craftsmen
Binder: Haddon Craftsmen

Owens not a good girl
McQueen not either, but she
redeems herself through exhibiting American
characteristics - hardworking, finds husband +
has nuclear family, is white
    - her profile is that of innocent victim -
      doing what she's supposed to do,
      is in place she's supposed to be
Owens, on other hand, is culpable victim-
    She asked for it
    - sexual promiscuity   - no husband or
                                nuclear family
    - drugs
    - welfare
    - desertion of kids
    - African American
completely un-American